ACHIEVING WELL-BEING FOR OPTIMUM SUCCESS

Achieving Well-being for Optimum Success

ANNA BARWICK

Anna Barwick

To David, for your unwavering love and support
To Karen and Jack, for always making me proud
And to my little sausage dog Conrad, for always being by my side

Copyright © 2023 by Anna Barwick

All rights reserved. No part of this book may be reproduced in any manner whatsoever without written permission except in the case of brief quotations embodied in critical articles and reviews.

First Printing, 2023

Legal Notice:
This book is copyright protected. This is only for personal use. You cannot amend, distribute, sell, use, quote or paraphrase any part or the content within this book without the consent of the author or copyright owner. Legal action will be pursued if this is breached.

Disclaimer Notice:
Please note the information contained within this book is for educational and entertainment purposes only. Every attempt has been made to provide accurate, up to date and reliable complete information. No warranties of any kind are expressed or implied. Readers acknowledge that the author is not engaging in the rendering of legal, financial, medical or professional advice. By reading this document, the reader agrees that under no circumstances are we responsible for any losses, direct or indirect, which are incurred as a result of the use of information contained within this document, including, but not limited to, errors, omissions, or inaccuracies.

CONTENTS

Dedication   iv

INTRODUCTION

1	Well-being	3
2	Engagement	8
3	Meaning	15
4	Accomplishment and Goal Setting	31
5	A Growth Mindset	44
6	Success	67
7	Motivation	91
8	Positive Emotions	111
9	Health	151

10	Stress	174
11	Positive Relationships	184
12	Conclusion	187

About The Author — 190

INTRODUCTION

Lying in a hospital theatre about to have your heart stopped and re-started with no actual certainty of coming out of it the other end is one of those events that can have a profound impact on how you view your life and reflect on what you have truly achieved and what is really important to you.

That was certainly the case for me, as the doctors tried for the second time to bring my heart and cardiovascular system back under control following a complete breakdown of my physical health and immune system after years of burning the candle at both ends in my drive to achieve academic success and build a successful career with complete focus only on these areas and to the detriment of my overall well-being.

Looking back, although the situation at the time involved a lengthy hospital stay and several years of recovery, to the detriment of the company I had striven to build up, I am now extremely grateful for the wake-up call it gave me, as it made me look at what is really important in life.

After spending my adult life striving for the sake of it, I realised that this does not bring true happiness and contentment, and I started looking for what is actually meaningful to me.

This journey of self-discovery led me to investigate positive psychology, and I found that it is possible to achieve even more success and perform even better by concentrating on the different aspects of well-being rather than blindly trying to achieve. And the added benefit of course, is that you are happier in the process!

My studies of positive psychology gave me the opportunity to work with my friend, the well-known positivity coach Sue Stone, and join her Sue Stone Foundation. I am very grateful to her for all her inspiration over the years.

Building my second successful company, this time an accountancy firm with a business coaching and consultancy arm, inspired me to change the focus of my career to help other entrepreneurs full-time to achieve more by working with them using positive psychology as well as my wealth of experience as an award-winning accountant and entrepreneur. I can honestly say that this opportunity has given my life the meaning it was previously lacking, and focusing on what gives me true purpose while using my natural talents and strengths has made me more successful while managing to achieve a work/life balance I previously never thought possible.

| 1 |

Well-being

What is well-being? Well-being is one of those words that we all know, but when we come to define it, we often struggle. Wellness is used interchangeably with well-being but is often used to refer to the health and fitness aspects of well-being only rather than the whole concept.

There have been many attempts at defining well-being, but because it is so multi-faceted, there is no single accepted definition. Professor Felicia Huppert puts it well in her definition that well-being is "your ability to feel good and function effectively". Well-being provides the tools to leverage the highs better and navigate the lows. With optimum well-being, we move beyond simply functioning to a state of flourishing and thriving and can focus on the good in life.

So, what is well-being not about? Achieving optimum well-being will not protect you from all the struggles in the world, but what it will do is give you the tools and ability to deal with it through the resilience it builds up in us. We should also note that facing challenges will not necessarily cause our well-being to suffer. Challenges are part of life, and they do not appear to reduce the levels of well-being we experience.

There is no single measure for our well-being, but in positive psychology we use six pillars, based on Professor Martin Seligman's findings, as the prerequisites for flourishing, namely:

- Positive emotions
- Engagement
- Relationships
- Meaning
- Accomplishment
- Health

But why is measuring well-being so important? We have already seen that there are a number of areas, or pillars, that come together to determine our level of well-being. But well-being is very subjective, and it is difficult to pinpoint areas where we could improve without considering the different components individually. If we can achieve optimum well-being, we benefit in a number of ways:

- Our performance improves, whether it be at work, in our studies or our leisure activities
- Our satisfaction with our relationships improves
- Our general physical health, and immune system, improves
- Our cardiovascular health improves
- Our life expectancy improves
- Our sleep improves
- Our mental and emotional health improves, reducing anxiety and depression
- Our stress levels improve
- We become more positive
- We feel happier
- We become more resilient
- Our energy levels improve
- We become more creative

As we can see, there are many reasons why we should strive for optimum well-being. But where do we start? Before we dive in, let me explain that in our enthusiasm for achieving all the benefits I listed above, we need to be realistic and appreciate that life is a series of ebbs and flows.

So, while there is nothing wrong with striving for optimum well-being, we need to balance it out by acknowledging this and accepting that this is how we learn and grow in life. If we are so obsessed with reaching an end goal, the danger is that instead of benefiting us, it actually causes more harm than good. A much healthier approach is acknowledging that it is a journey rather than a destination and enjoying every small improvement we can make.

Fortunately, there are lots of things we can do to improve our overall well-being, and the rest of the book will explore the six pillars and the more important sub-sections and how we can improve on these individual areas to achieve a better overall result.

Measuring well-being

A good place to start is by measuring our current well-being and doing a well-being survey to discover how we currently fare in the six main areas. The PERMAH Wellbeing Survey (permahsurvey.com) is a free survey that will give you a lot of information about your levels in each category.

A simple exercise for assessing each pillar yourself is the PERMAH Wheel. You use it to register your score as a basis for which areas need improvement. One thing to bear in mind is that, with both the PERMAH Survey and also the PERMAH Wheel, there is no right or wrong. The score is simply a reflection of your perceived level of well-being.

For each of the sections, score yourself on a scale of 1 to 5, where:

1. Struggling
2. Getting by
3. Doing ok
4. Doing well
5. Thriving

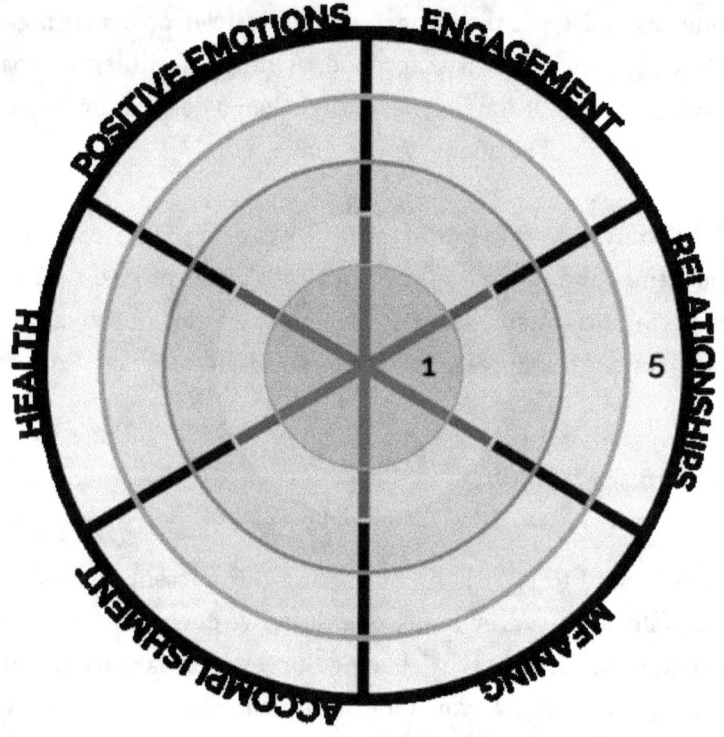

POSITIVE EMOTIONS	feeling joy, excitement, awe, gratitude, amusement
ENGAGEMENT	being absorbed in an activity, using your strengths, being in flow
RELATIONSHIPS	connections with others, romantic, work, friends
MEANING	what is important to you, finding your "why"
ACCOMPLISHMENT	your progress towards your goals and success
HEALTH	nutrition, exercise, sleep, relaxation, meditation

When you score yourself on the wheel, bear in mind that virtually nobody will score 5 in all six categories. Instead, look at it objectively as an indication of where you could work towards improving your overall well-being, and then concentrate on that area.

And the good news is that you do not have to be extraordinary to get extraordinary results. When you look at the happiest and most successful people, you will find that they have a number of characteristics in common, and most of them can be learnt, which is what the rest of this book will focus on.

| 2 |

Engagement

Engagement in terms of well-being is about using our strengths and talents to engage in activities that inspire us and fulfil our potential. If we can engage in activities that stimulate and motivate us sufficiently to completely absorb our attention, we are said to be in flow. This state of flow is the ultimate we aim for in terms of engagement.

Being in flow

So, it is all well and good telling you that for ultimate engagement, you need to be in flow, but how do you know when you have achieved this, and also, how do you know how to achieve it in the first place? Being in flow is when you, according to Csíkszentmihályi, experience some or all of the following:

1. An activity that is intrinsically rewarding
2. There are clear goals for the activity, which challenge you but are still attainable
3. You are completely focused on the activity
4. You feel personally in control of the situation and the outcome

5. You are not feeling self-conscious as you are completely absorbed in the activity, and you feel serene
6. You receive immediate feedback
7. There is a balance between your skills and the challenge you are presented with
8. You lose awareness of your physical needs
9. You are concentrating fully on the activity
10. You lose all track of time

That is clearly a long list, but think about what you really enjoy doing, perhaps in your leisure time. Maybe you enjoy a concert or sports game so much that time positively flies by. That is a typical example of being in flow.

Why is achieving being in flow essential to well-being? When we are in flow, we become happier and more productive, and our life is more rewarding. The best way to get in flow is to use our talents and strengths. Ultimately, this leads to our chances of success in life improving, as we will see throughout this book.

Motivation

We have seen what engagement is, but why should we be concerned with it? There has been a lot of research done on what motivates people, and one of the main factors they found was that individuals with high engagement are more likely to be naturally motivated. What this means to us is that if we can increase our engagement, we become more willing to take responsibility for our results, commit to our goals and be motivated to overcome the challenges we face. The benefits of being motivated include:

- Greater life satisfaction
- Greater levels of well-being

- You are more likely to achieve your goals
- Greater levels of self-belief and self-esteem

We explore motivation in more detail in a later chapter.

Productivity and performance

In terms of work productivity and performance, companies with engaged employees have been found to be 21% more productive and 22% more profitable. Research has also found that engaging workers can reduce staff turnover by as much as 65% and increase customer ratings by up to 10%. From an employer's perspective, it is, therefore, a no-brainer to ensure you have an engaged workforce, but for the individual entrepreneur, it is also clear to see that by increasing your engagement, you will become more productive and profitable in your work, and ultimately be more successful. Increasing workforce engagement involves making sure they feel included and fully understand the importance of the part they play in the ultimate success of the business.

How can we increase engagement?

The best way to increase engagement is to become aware of your strengths, i.e., what you are good at, and use these strengths in the tasks you undertake. Sadly, over 90% of people are not aware of what their strengths are, so by finding out and using this discovery, you are straight away putting yourself in the top 10% of people!

This concept of concentrating on our strengths is, to a large extent, likely to be in complete contrast with what you have been told all your life. Most of us were told at school to improve on our weaker subjects rather than perfecting our strengths. It is likely that this concept has followed you throughout your adult life and is almost ingrained in your thought pattern.

The positive psychology approach is to focus on your strengths because you are likely to be more engaged, and using our strengths counteracts the negative aspects of our lives and allows us to build on the positive. That doesn't mean we should ignore our weaknesses, but by focusing on using our strengths, we actually improve our weaknesses at the same time.

We have all got strengths, and these strengths make us unique and provide us with the opportunity to excel. We can develop our strengths by using our unique talents to achieve goals. Using our strengths allows us to work in our zone of genius. But we have already seen that more than 90% of the population do not know their strengths, so how can we find out what ours are? A very simple way is to think about what you really enjoy doing because it is likely to be because you are using your strengths. Another way is to think about what your friends and colleagues come to you for. Again, it is likely to be something that uses your strengths because they have spotted your talents.

A more formal way of finding out your strengths is to take a survey to determine them. There are two types of strengths surveys. One focuses on your natural talents and how you can develop them to succeed in what you do. The other focuses on your character strengths, sometimes also called personality traits. Although the focus differs, there is likely to be some overlap between the strengths that the surveys identify.

Gallup Clifton Strengthsfinder

(www.gallup.com)

This survey is used to discover your natural talents. Talents are the source of our true potential and power, and when we develop them, they become our strengths. Developing them takes time, practice and hard work, but we are rewarded with improved performance and productivity, and we become happier when we build our strengths.

The Gallup Strengthsfinder is a paid survey, and you can choose between a full report of your 34 strengths or a shorter report of your top 5 strengths. Whichever one you decide to go for, prioritising the top 5 strengths is the best starting point. And if you do not feel you want to invest in a paid survey, although I highly recommend it, there are other free surveys available that will give you very similar results, but generally without detailed reports on how to maximise your potential.

VIA (Values in Action) Character Strengths

(www.viacharacter.org)

As the name implies, this free survey is used to discover your character strengths and values.
We will go into these in detail in the next chapter on Meaning.

Benefits of using our strengths

Instead of spending our time and energy on improving our weaknesses and concentrating on preventing failure, we can now concentrate on our strengths and use them to succeed.

Research by Gallup has found that if we develop and use our talents:

- We are six times more engaged and happier in our work
- And three times more likely to have an excellent quality of life
- If we use our strengths every day, our productivity improves by 14%

So there are plenty of reasons we should develop and use our strengths. You may have heard it referred to as working in our zone of genius, which is an excellent way of looking at it.

How do we learn to use our strengths?

Now we know what our strengths are and why we should be focusing on them, it is time to look at how we can use our strengths more so we can become more confident and productive. A good place to start, now you know what your top 5 strengths are, is to keep a **Strengths Usage Journal** for the next month. In it record:

1. A description of all the activities that give you energy, whether positive or negative
2. The emotions you felt while doing the activity
3. How much you enjoyed the activity
4. How energised you felt doing the activity
5. And finally, which strengths (from your survey) that you may have been using

Journalling like this makes you think about how you approach what you do, rather than just the task you do itself. The next step is to try to incorporate the activities you enjoy the most into your life as much as possible. And make sure to read and absorb the specific suggestions in the report on how to maximise your potential for each of your top 5 strengths.

We started the chapter by explaining the concept of being in flow. Now you know your strengths, you can revisit the activities that you identified cause you to be in flow and consider the relationship between the two. A useful way to build on your strengths is to undertake as many activities as possible where you are in flow.

Introducing Mindfulness

This book keeps coming back to the importance of mindfulness for optimum well-being. For now, I want to highlight how mindfulness can help us identify when we are using our strengths.

Mindfulness means being present in everything we do and not getting lost in thinking about what has happened in the past or may happen in the future. It is also about being non-reactive and non-judgemental and simply being an observer of what is happening in the now.

What being mindful does, in relation to engagement and strengths use, is to allow us to observe when we use our strengths in our everyday life and what we use them for. This can form a solid base for considering further how else we can put our strengths to good use in other areas of our life and work.

| 3 |

Meaning

The concept of finding your why, or meaning in your life, is fundamental to optimum well-being, and I will explore it in this chapter, along with an introduction to goal setting and achievement. A happy life is a fulfilled life, and finding fulfilment involves doing things that bring you deeper purpose and meaning.

Meaning is how you make sense of your life and what you are doing now and have done in the past that makes life valuable and worthwhile to you. To live a meaningful life, we need to have a sense of belonging and purpose. In turn, when we are living a meaningful life, we have greater longevity and are more positive, optimistic, and motivated, and our lives are enriched.

And the good news is that we all have the opportunity to create a meaningful life!

Purpose

One of the driving forces that have encouraged recent research into personal development and social behaviour is purpose. As we begin to become gradually aware of who we are, we feel the need to discover more about our existence and our life's purpose. The best approach to adopt when delving into and discussing the concept of purpose is to know what purpose is and how it is different from goals.

Purpose refers to defining the goals in life that provide you with personal meaning. Purpose directs your decisions and goals by guiding the use of your finite personal resources. Instead of governing your behaviour, purpose offers you direction, not dissimilar to a compass that guides a navigator. Following your purpose is purely optional, but there are significant benefits to doing so.

Living in accordance with your purpose makes you a self-sustaining force, and that aids goal pursuit and goal attainment. Therefore, purpose is critical for helping us to organise our lives and develop persistence that resonates across time and context.

The Difference Between Purpose and Goals

Even though they are mentioned continuously together in conversational context and research, purpose and goals are not the same.

Goals are more precise and focus on a more specific endpoint and serve to guide our behaviour either toward or away from the endpoint.

Purpose, on the other hand, is a broader component that influences behaviour and stimulates the goals. Purpose doesn't point you toward a designated outcome, but instead, it motivates you to be goal-oriented. Unlike goals, which have terminal results, purpose and values merely provide you with the general direction in life.

Another way to look at purpose is to view it as the goal manager. If you have a purpose in your life, you are better able to move seamlessly from goal to goal and even have the capacity to manage multiple goals at once.

On the other hand, if you do not have a purpose in life, you may be successful in achieving a single goal but will find it extremely challenging to identify your next target. Therefore, goals act as the centre point and are produced and inspired by your purpose in life.

The Dimensions of Purpose

Purpose is found on a three-dimensional scale consisting of strength, scope, and awareness. Scope refers to the extent to which your purpose affects your life. For example, a goal that influences all your actions, thoughts, and emotions is said to have a broad scope. A purpose with a narrow scope is more organised but doesn't impact a greater range of behaviours in comparison with a purpose with a full reach.

Strength, in regard to purpose, is the tendency for the purpose to influence your actions, thoughts, and emotions on the domains relevant to its scope. A definite purpose powerfully influences appropriate behaviours to your purpose. Combined with scope, strength dictates the extent to which your purpose will affect your health, longevity, and well-being. For instance, a purpose that is characterised by great power and a broader scope will have a more pronounced effect on your life. Additionally, a strong and broad purpose brings resilience to obstacles and barriers you may face during your journey.

Awareness reflects the extent that a person is knowledgeable and can articulate their purpose. Both scope and strength strongly influence it. Consider the analogy of gravity for a moment. On earth, the force of gravity is broader in scope but weak in its impact. As we live our lives, we do not pay attention to the gravitational forces that are keeping our feet firmly planted. However, if we were to be taken to Jupiter, which has twice as much gravitational force, our awareness of the force of gravity would increase substantially.

Behaviours consistent with purpose can be activated to provide motivation for action. When you are aware of a purpose, it will take you less effort to pursue it than if you were completely unaware.

Finding your passion

Most people try to justify their failures and uncertainties in life to not having enough passion in one thing or another. This causes them to be in a continuous cycle of pursuing boring and uninteresting things.

Contrary to popular belief, discovering what you love is not as challenging as it may seem. Passion is not a precious commodity that is reserved for a select few. Rather, it is a gift that everybody has been blessed with. The only thing we need to do to discover our passion is to have the right attitude. Work is supposed to be fun, so you must take the time to explore what you enjoy. Rather than viewing yourself as hopeless because you have yet to discover your passion, begin to visualise yourself being surrounded by endless possibilities. The reality is that the only limit you have to be doing what you love is a lack of imagination.

Allow yourself opportunities

The reason why you are not pursuing what you love might be that you do not believe you deserve to be passionate about what you do. However, everyone has the right to be passionate in their pursuits in life. You need to wake up excited about your life because you have every right to do so. When you permit yourself to pursue what you do passionately, you will be in a much better position to help others as well. You need to modify your mental picture if you want to resonate, accept, and love what you do. The moment you can align your identity with your passion, it will become much easier for you to find fulfilment in the things you do in life.

Allow yourself to explore

You must understand that there is a whole spectrum of possibilities regarding your fulfilment and enjoyment of what you do. At one end of the spectrum is the work you hate and cannot do under any circumstance. The other end of the spectrum is the work you love, and the mere thought brings you excitement and energy. Between these two points is a huge range of work that bores you, work that makes you feel indifferent, work that challenges and stimulates you, and tasks that make you come alive with excitement.

The aim is to move in the direction of the spectrum that makes you come alive. As you pursue what you love, you will come across options that will lead you to your ultimate life's purpose. The more you seek that work that excites you, the more efficient you will become at filtering out everything else that tends to drain your energy and distracts you from your desired outcome.

Look for opportunities

The opportunities to do what we love are right in front of us. Unfortunately, we tend to think that we cannot make a meaningful living from what we do. When you change your perspective, you might find the things that you have been looking down on are the most fascinating and exciting.

To figure out what we are passionate about, most people fail to ask themselves powerful questions. You need to give yourself time and let go of other activities to allow yourself to engage with your passion. Often, we let other things take precedence at the expense of exploring the things that excite us. For you to succeed in finding your passion, you need to set aside quality time to figure out what makes you excited. Some of the questions that you need to ask yourself that can lead you to discover your purpose and passions are:

- What would you do, even if you will not get paid for it?
- What are the gifts or skills that you can share with the world?
- When in your life do you feel most creative?
- What comes naturally to you?
- What have you accomplished in the past that was successful?

Asking yourself these questions will awaken your subconscious mind and allow you to start searching within yourself to discover your passion.

Live your life with the end in mind

What does it mean to live your life with the end in mind? It means that you have a picture of the end as a point of reference by which you examine everything in life. Every part of your life can be aptly observed in the context of your entire life and what really matters to you. By keeping the end in mind, you can be sure that whatever you do on any particular day will not change your overall purpose.

Just like a pilot beginning his journey with a destination in mind, so should your life. This means that you should know where you want to go so that you can better understand where you are now and the steps that you will need to take to move in the right direction.

Often in life, we find ourselves attaining hollow victories. We realise that success came at the expense of things that were far more important and valuable. People from every profession and all walks of life struggle to achieve a high income, more recognition, or a certain level of professional competence. However, they may not realise that their ambition to achieve these lofty goals can potentially blind them to the things that matter the most, and unfortunately, they do not understand this until it is too late. Your true definition of success will become clear when you consider what you want to be said about you at the end of your life.

I certainly found this to be true when I had a complete breakdown of my immune system and ended up hospitalised, nearly dying twice, after years of burning the candle both ends while blindly racing along on a path to achieve without any clear idea of why I wanted to achieve the success. It was simply that I was driven by success. But lying in a hospital theatre, having my heart stopped and restarted for the second time to try to get my cardiovascular system back under control, I realised exactly the importance of this exercise, and I am sure what got me through and allowed me to come out on the other side was the realisation that I had more to do in life. I did not want to be remembered just for having achieved high academic scores and built a multi-million-pound business. There had to be more to life, and I was determined to live long enough to find out what that was.

So, as I started my slow road to recovery, with time on my hands due to my enforced break, I started searching for my why, only at the time, I did not know that was what I was doing. During my voyage of self-discovery, I found positive psychology, and I learned all that I am sharing in this book. First and foremost, I learned that well-being and achievement are not an either/or. It is possible to live your best life with meaning while still being immensely successful in both work and life in general. I realised that over the years, what had brought me real joy was when I was sharing my experience and helping others progress, and that this brought real meaning to my life. This made me able to, rather than feel those years of striving had been a form of failure, be grateful for having had the experiences and years of learning that now enabled me to do something that is meaningful. In doing so, I have become even more successful than when I was aimlessly chasing hollow goals, and now I am achieving happiness and well-being in the process.

None of us is immortal! There will come a time when we shall leave this world, and whether you have lived your purpose or not, your time will be out with no possibility of a bonus. Living with the end in mind will help you to align your life with your purpose. You need to live your life in a way that, in the end, everyone will have something positive to say about your contributions, achievements, and character. Having this perspective in life will enhance your personal understanding of your purpose and how to go about accomplishing it.

Values

In the previous chapter, I introduced the subject of strengths and how different surveys can help you find your unique strengths. The second of the surveys, the VIA (Values in Action) survey, looks at your character strengths.

Values are closely connected with your meaning and purpose. When we live in harmony with our values, our levels of well-being improve. Values are like an internal compass that helps us choose the right path and know when we are steering off that path. They give our life meaning and purpose. The VIA survey will have helped you discover your top character strengths. It also classifies these into six categories, or virtues:

Wisdom and knowledge. This includes the values:

- Curiosity
- Creativity
- Judgement
- Love of learning

- Perspective

Transcendence. This includes the values:

- Appreciation of beauty and excellence
- Gratitude
- Hope
- Humour
- Spirituality

Courage. This includes the values:

- Perseverance
- Bravery
- Honesty
- Zest

Humanity. This includes the values:

- Love
- Kindness
- Social intelligence

Temperance. This includes the values:

- Forgiveness
- Humility
- Prudence
- Self-regulation

Justice. This includes the values:

- Teamwork
- Fairness
- Leadership

By identifying your top character strengths in the above categories, you can explore further what your values are. Our values are influenced by family, relationships, and community, and identifying what values are truly meaningful to and what we align with takes time and a lot of self-reflection. Questions you can ask yourself include who you admire and what their qualities are, and also how you want to show up in the world.

Do not let others shape your life and values

In your life, if you cannot develop a sense of self-awareness, you are empowering other people outside your circle of influence to shape your life by default. If you want to awaken your true calling, then you need to stop living the scripts that are handed to you by your family, friends, colleagues, and other people's agenda. These scripts have their origins in people, not principles and cannot lead you to your purpose.

Writing your own script

Since we already have a lot of scripts handed over to us, the process of writing our own scripts can be seen more as a rescripting process. In developing your self-awareness, you may well discover some ineffective scripts that are deeply embedded in you which are completely different from your values. You are responsible for writing new scripts that are more effective with your deepest values and principles.

Develop your own mission statement

The most effective way to integrate the end into your journey is to develop a personal mission statement. Your mission statement should focus on what you want to be, what you want to do, and the values upon which your character and achievements are founded.

To write a meaningful personal mission statement, you must start at the centre of your circle of influence. The centre is what consists of the lens through which you view the world. It is what enables you to deal with your values and visions and helps you mentally create the life you were meant to live.

Positive visualisation

Creative visualisation is instrumental in achieving your goals and accomplishing your tasks. When it comes to our internal mental creation, our brains cannot differentiate between the real and the imagined. The imagery you create in your mind has a real and tangible effect on your body. When you place your personal belief in the process of imagination, you can attain your goals and live a purposeful life.

Building a foundation

Just like any process, visualisation requires a foundation. If you bring to your memory the thoughts that occupied your mind before past failed or successful events, you will discover that your thought pattern led you to act in a certain manner which attracted the corresponding events and circumstances. This proves that your thoughts can create great changes with the help of visualisation and imagery.

Creative visualisation

Creative visualisation is a mental technique that uses the power of imagination and the mind to make changes in your life and drive you toward your purpose. With creative visualisation, you can shape your character, circumstances, and habits, as well as attract the opportunities and the things that you most desire in your life.

The thoughts that are repeated most will affect your subconscious mind and make things happen. The subconscious controls your desires, habits, reactions, and actions. They also attract similar circumstances. Your imagination will create mental scenarios of certain events and incidences in your life through creative visualisation.

The more you feed your thoughts, the stronger they get. Your imagination is your most important and powerful tool of creative visualisation. Through imagination, we develop the cars, computers, and buildings we see today.

Integrating creative visualisation into your life

To live a purposeful, driven life, you need to bring in visualisation. Just like learning how to drive a car or play a musical instrument, visualisation will require patience and persistence. If you want to experience the full benefits of visualisation, you need to put in the discipline as well as the time and practice until you perfect the process.

The length of time that it will take for you to start seeing results will fully depend on the vividness of your imagination, as well as your own level of determination. Experts suggest that you practice for 15 to 20 minutes every day. As you start to master the skill and become more comfortable with the technique, you can reduce the time to just a few minutes a day.

Research indicates that for your visualisation to work, it is best done in conjunction with a relaxation technique. The studies showed that when your body is relaxed, your mind is also comfortable and not so much under conscious control, giving it the freedom to daydream.

There are many techniques that can be used in visualisation and imagery to call the desired feeling and provide you with a direction of purpose. One of the most common methods is known as guided visualisation, and it involves visualising a goal you want to achieve and then imagining yourself going through the process of achieving that goal.

Since thoughts, when combined with mental images and emotions, will lead to actions and results, creative visualisation can overcome the practical barriers to the attainment of your purpose. By repeating the same thoughts, every day, you will program your subconscious mind to bring the visualisation into reality.

Being Proactive

As an individual, you are directly responsible for your own life. Your behaviour is a sum of all the decisions you have made, not your conditions. You are the only person with the initiative and the responsibility to turn your life around and make things happen.

People who are proactive are conscious of their purpose, and they know that the conditions and circumstances around them are not to blame, but it is rather their own behaviour that holds them back from awakening their true purpose in life.

Your behaviour is a direct product of your conscious choices that are based on your value systems. By nature, we are all proactive beings, and in the event our lives are conditioned by the circumstances around us, it is because we have made the decision, consciously, to empower those things to control us.

The opposite of being proactive is reactive. When you are reactive, you are affected by the physical environment more than your own value system. For example, when the weather around a reactive person is good, then everything else is fine, and their attitude and performance is not affected. However, if the weather changes, so does their position and performance.

Proactive people are masters of their own destinies and purpose. Whether it rains or not, it makes absolutely no difference to proactive people. Because their value systems drive them, they will continue to produce quality work.

If you want to live a purposeful life, you need to lessen your impulses to a value that is central to your existence. Even though external stimuli may influence you from time to time, your response to these stimuli should be value-based. To remain on track in pursuing your goals and life's purpose, you need to own up to and acknowledge that the choices you have made thus far in your life have made you into who you are today.

Taking Initiative

Our basic nature is programmed to act and not be acted upon. We ultimately have the power to choose our responses to the circumstances around us. Taking the initiative has nothing to do with being aggressive, obnoxious, or pushy, but rather it has everything to do with being able to recognise our personal responsibility to make things happen. Too many people stand around waiting for something to happen or for someone else to take care of their affairs.

If you want to find a good job that centres around your passion, one that you will enjoy for a long time, you must be proactive and generate creative solutions to the problems that you or your company face. You must seize the initiative so that you can do whatever takes to get the job done.

There is a substantial difference between people who take the initiative and those who do not. Life is fair in the sense that everyone has the opportunity to steer their lives toward their purpose or destiny. However, if you do not allow the opportunities in front of you to prevail, those around you will use you to accomplish their own purposes.

Regardless of your personality, you can create a proactive culture in your life by combining your creativity and resourcefulness. You do not have any excuses for being at the mercy of the environment. Instead, you can take the initiative and accomplish your life's purpose.

Realise your own proactivity

A great way to become more aware of your degree of proactivity is to analyse where you focus your resources. There are a lot of concerns that each of us has in our lives. To separate the things we have no specific emotional or mental involvement in, you can create a circle of concern.

When you begin to examine those things in your circle of concern, it will start to become clear that there are certain things that you have no control over and others that you might be able to do something about. The things you discover you have control over can be regrouped further into a smaller circle of influence.

When you can determine your allocation of time and energy between the circle of concern and the sphere of influence, you can then discover the extent of your proactivity. Those who are proactive in their lives care about their purpose in life and focus their efforts on those things that are in their circle of influence. They only concentrate on the things that they can do something about.

On the other hand, reactive people become much more engrossed in the circle of concern. They focus more on the weaknesses of others, the problems with the environment, and the circumstances that are well beyond their control. This results in a confused and purposeless life that is based on blaming and accusing attitudes, reactive language, and increased feelings of victimisation.

If you find yourself working in the circle of concern and focusing on the things within that circle, you will not accomplish anything. However, if you can shift your focus and start working in your sphere of influence, you will create positive energy that will change you and that will influence your subsequent actions.

It is inspiring to realise that you can powerfully affect your overall situation by choosing how you respond to circumstances. When you can change a section of your chemical formula, you can alter the nature of the results. If you want to improve your situation and find your purpose in life, you need to concentrate on the things that you have control over.

| 4 |

Accomplishment and Goal Setting

Accomplishment is about successfully achieving what we set out to do. It is one of the pillars Professor Martin Seligman identified as fundamental to our well-being. It involves working towards and reaching a particular goal, mastering a task and having the self-motivation to accomplish what we set out to do.

Hope Theory

Hope Theory originates in the work of Professor Charles R Snyder, who researched and wrote many works on the impact of hope on our health, work, education and personal meaning. It is very closely linked with goal setting. Hope is the state of mind that helps you navigate life's twists and turns and which keeps you moving forward when faced with challenges. Hope is not simply about feeling happy, it is a human survival mechanism, and we cannot reach optimum well-being without it.

Professor Snyder identified three things that make up Hope Theory:

1. Goals – approaching life in a goal-oriented way
2. Pathways – finding different ways to achieve our goals
3. Agency – believing that you can initiate changes and achieve these goals

He found that when any of these components is missing, it is unlikely that we will reach our desired goals. By contrast, people high in hope:

- Are more resilient
- Have less stress and anxiety
- Have greater performance and engagement
- Have more meaningful lives
- Are more motivated
- Set higher and clearer goals

He also characterised hopeful thinkers as those who can set clear goals, imagine a number of pathways towards achieving those goals, and who are able to persevere when obstacles get in the way of the goals, and that the goals we set must be of sufficient value to warrant sustained, conscious thought about them.

Hope Theory has been used to develop a Hope Map, a goal-setting method which follows six steps, and which I find extremely useful when it comes to goal-setting and which I recommend using in your goal setting:

1. **Set goal.** The goal may be long-term or short-term.
   You should use the SMART mnemonic (Specific, Measurable, Attainable, Relevant and Time-bound) to set your goal, to ensure it is clear, and so that you know what you are trying to achieve. Ensure it is attainable, yet at the same time, will challenge you. Too easy or too hard will be demotivating.

2. **Find pathways to achieve your goal.** This follows point 2 above in Professor Snyder's Hope Theory.

   It is based on "pathways thinking" which refers to the belief that you can find workable routes to your goal.

   For this step, you should make a list of the pathways you need to take to achieve your goal.

3. **Identify the obstacles and barriers to achieving your goal.**

   It is unlikely that we will accomplish a goal without coming up against obstacles.

   One of the reasons I find Hope Mapping so powerful is that, unlike traditional goal-setting theories, which were good at setting goals but provided no help with overcoming challenges, here we are being proactive and considering all possible obstacles and barriers before they even happen.

   For each of the pathways located above, give yourself time to consider what obstacles you are likely to come up against so that you are aware before you even start.

4. **Identify pathways around each of the obstacles you identified above**

   Now we are going to concentrate on how we are going to overcome the potential obstacles by spending some time finding ways to overcome the obstacles you identified in step 3.

   For each obstacle, think of at least one way you can overcome it. This may mean adding additional pathways or steps to get around the obstacle.

5. **Think of your why for this goal.** Make a note of why you want to achieve this goal and how you will feel if you do not achieve it.

   This will be what you will refer to when things get hard and your motivation fades a little.

   By reminding yourself why you must carry on and achieve your goal, you will reignite the motivation that made you set the goal in the first place.

6. **Identify your support network.** All goals will require a support network of some kind, and now is when you need to ensure yours is in place. A support network for a work goal may be the availability of colleagues and resources you need to draw on to achieve the goal. For a personal goal, it may be the support of your partner or friends that will be there to act as your cheerleaders and encourage you on your journey to achieving your goal.

Setting personal goals that fuel your purpose

Setting goals is an important foundation for awakening your true purpose and finding success. This is because goals help us to concentrate our actions and energy on the end result while measuring our progress concerning the goals that we have set.

However, many people acknowledge that a gap exists between setting goals and being able to develop and communicate important goals that produce sustained action while generating transformational results. It has been proven that there are clear links between motivation, performance, and goal-setting. Along with setting goals for yourself, you should also use goal setting as a tool to create a sense of direction and purpose. The environment of goal setting is crucial because it provides the conditions necessary to be effective in all your pursuits.

The importance of goals in living a meaningful life

Goals reflect your purpose and point you toward the expected quality, quantity, and performance. As a process, setting goals always creates discrepancies because of the gap between our current situation and the desired future state. Additionally, the process of setting goals affects our overall level of motivation, our belief system, and our capacity to perform. The discrepancy that is created by goal-setting should be interpreted as the catalyst that will motivate us to persistently strive to reach our goal.

Three conditions need to be met if the process of setting goals is going to be motivating:

1. You need to have a commitment to your part in the process. This means that you need to have a "whatever it takes" attitude to achieve your goals. If you have a lack of commitment, you will have a lack of motivation.
2. You also need to set specific and unambiguous goals. This will make it easier to access your progress and adjust accordingly.
3. Finally, you need to have goal-directed behaviour and happiness.

A goal-oriented action is a critical element of the goal-setting theory. If you do not have goal-directed action, it will be impossible for you to achieve your purpose.

Harnessing the power of setting goals

There are powerful tools that you can use to put goal setting to work. These tools take into consideration human dynamics as they help us to generate goals that will lead us to purposeful and effective behaviour.

- *Self-efficacy*

  The concept of self-efficacy is extremely important to setting and achieving goals. Efficacy is the belief you hold about your ability to perform a certain task. These beliefs will affect the way we set goals, as well as the choices that we make about the activities we engage in. Efficacy can also refer to the measure of how much effort we are willing to expend and the length of time we will persist in the face of challenges or failure.

  Setting short-term sub-goals will raise your self-efficacy as

compared to setting only long-term goals. Your goals should be challenging and clear, and they should consist of a target and a timeframe. The level of self-confidence should be commensurate with the level of goal difficulty.

- **Task complexity**

When you set goals for complex tasks, you want to ensure that you include short-term goals because they provide you with immediate guidelines and incentives for better performance. Long-term goals alone can be too far removed and difficult for you to connect with. Goal setting requires realistic expectations and appropriate strategies to accomplish the task.

- **Goal commitment**

When you are committed to your goals, the relationship between your performance and the goal increases. As the goals become more difficult, the level of commitment must be raised to match the effort that is required to attain those goals. The two main factors that are needed in enhancing your goal commitment are prioritisation and self-belief. You have to believe that you will attain the goals you have set, as well as make achieving your goals a priority. To succeed in achieving your goals, you must link them to the bigger picture.

- **Feedback**

For goal setting to be effective, it must be paired with appropriate feedback. Timely feedback will provide you with the necessary information about whether your picture of reality is properly aligned with what you need to achieve your goals. When you receive ongoing feedback, it indicates that you are paying attention to the progress you are making in achieving the goals you have set.

- **Satisfaction**

Satisfaction in your life increases when you exceed your goals. As you increase your number of successes, your overall satisfaction also grows. To incorporate satisfaction when setting your goals, you need to set challenging goals that improve your interest. This will help you discover the pleasurable aspects of accomplishing your tasks.

Self-management

An important process in purposeful living is self-management. Self-management is what helps in directing and establishing you on the right path toward your destiny. In its simplest definition, self-management refers to the planning, organising, directing, and coordinating of various aspects of your life so that you achieve your life's purpose.

To effectively manage yourself, you must possess a strong and independent will. Self-management is a necessary skill in today's complex world if we want to recognise our hidden potential. We need to master effective self-management principles if we are going to maximise our skills to be able to come up with solutions to our daily challenges. Self-management helps you control your life and build meaningful interpersonal relationships in the pursuit of your passion and purpose. Through self-management, you can break through your limits and live a fulfilled life.

The four rules of self-management

If you want to become an effective person who knows how to manage your affairs and take control of your life, there are four rules that you need to observe. These rules will act as your personal guiding system as you work toward discovering your purpose:

1. The first thing that you must do is map your life. This step will allow you to understand yourself regarding who you are, where you are coming from, and where you are going. This will provide you with an orientation of purpose and direction. Mapping

out your life is at the core of every success that you will achieve in your life.
2. The second rule that you need to observe is to review your assumptions. Everyone has a belief system and a unique perspective that is used to assess ourselves. Some of the assumptions that you hold can hinder your journey to achieving your life goals and finding happiness. Reviewing the assumptions that you hold will allow you to look inside yourself. We will look at this in more detail in the next chapter.
3. Once you have reviewed your assumptions, the third rule you need to observe is to organise yourself and your potential to achieve your desired goals. Without this self-organisation, even the skills that you possess have the potential to be diminished.
4. The fourth rule is to develop your abilities, which is closely linked with self-organisation. This includes the development and improvement of your imagination, introspection, and willpower, along with other skills. These will greatly enhance your capacity to express yourself.

Willpower and integrity

Willpower refers to the ability to make decisions and choices and act in accordance with them. It is a proactive approach to carrying out the plan you have developed for your life. The extent of your personal integrity measures the degree of willpower development in your life. The higher the level of your integrity, the more independent your will. Integrity is simply your ability to make commitments and follow through with them.

Effective self-management requires that you prioritise things in your life. As a self-manager, your discipline to organise the various aspects of your life should come from within your own value system. Being independent will give you the power to do something even when you do not want to, as long as it is in line with your underlying values.

To develop your willpower, you must start by setting up and achieving small resolutions. This can give you the momentum and the zeal to move on and take on more substantial assignments. You can boost your willpower through clarity of purpose, the priority of purpose, good planning, and determination.

Time management

Another essential self-management skill is your ability to manage your time. Time management skills help you to organise and execute your tasks based on your priorities. Each of us has the same number of hours, and how we use them determines the extent of our success or failure.

To manage the time that you have, you need to prioritise and discipline yourself. Whenever the tasks overwhelm you, you should learn to delegate effectively to reliable and capable people. This will give you more time to focus on your remaining tasks.

One tool I have used for years is to spend 30-45 minutes on a Sunday afternoon/early evening planning the following week. Because it is easy for this to become a chore, I make this an enjoyable event, where I sit down, do some mindfulness medication with aromatherapy candles, and then proceed to plan my week. This way, it is something I look forward to doing, and the whole concept of time management becomes a positive event.

I start by noting the things I must do, such as meetings and deadlines. Then I note the things I should do and, finally, the things I would like to get done but are less critical. My self-care routine is one of the non-negotiables under must do. By planning a week ahead, I get an overview of where I am, but without looking so far into the future that something will likely come along and derail the plans.

Overcoming negativity

The ability to move through challenges and difficulties and still maintain hope, wellness of mind, and positive coping methods is known as resilience. People who possess resilience can keep their focus and emerge stronger after going through difficult situations.

As you move toward your purpose, you will realise that you will face many challenges that will require you to have self-confidence and new coping skills to make it through to the other side. Resilience can help you overcome any negative element that tries to take you off course.

Individuals who are resilient usually display certain personality characteristics that influence the manner in which they view problems and how they solve them. Resilience is affected by some of the following personality qualities.

Optimism

When you believe that things will get better and that the current difficulties and challenges that you are currently facing will be solved, it means that you have optimism.

Independence

Independence refers to your ability to make decisions in your life and order your own actions without having to rely on other people to tell you what to do.

Responsibility

This refers to the calmness and inner peace that comes when you believe that you can do something to change the unfortunate circumstances that you may find yourself in from time to time.

In order for you to learn to overcome negativity, you have to learn how to train yourself to think positively, even when you are going through a difficult and stressful situation. You have the innate ability to change your negative thoughts into more positive ones and find the humour in things, even when everything seems to be going wrong.

While the past may have been bad, and your present situation is not the greatest, this doesn't mean that your future opportunities are going to be jeopardised unless, however, you allow the situation to do so. Your purpose in life may not be on a straight path, and that is why you have to overcome negativity and focus on the final goal.

How to improve your resilience

For you to overcome challenges in your life, you have to take deliberate steps to enhance your resilience levels. The first thing that you can do is to start to incorporate positive affirmations into your daily life.

Words are extremely powerful! Whatever you say has the potential to become a reality. When you speak positively about your life, you will be amazed at how quickly it turns around for the better.

Life is not always going to give you easy options. You have to strive and make it purposeful irrespective of the immediate circumstances. When you increase your determination to go against all the odds, you will build your resilience.

When you learn to establish and enhance your communication skills, you will be able to express yourself better and get the help you need when faced with difficult situations.

When it comes to some of the challenges you meet, you will find that you need someone to listen to you and a shoulder to lean on. With better communication, you will find it easier to seek advice when facing a crisis concerning your purpose.

Decision-making is an integral process in your daily life. When you face challenges and problems, your ability to conduct yourself with an open mind can help you to get through your problems regardless of their difficulty. These skills will help you to manoeuvre and maintain focus on your ultimate goals and life's purpose.

Resilience and our brain

Modern science has taught us about the biological processes of the brain and how it affects our reasoning, determination, and ability to pull through difficult situations. Some parts of the brain produce chemicals that boost our happiness levels while others bring about anxiety and fear.

To be mentally, physically, and behaviourally healthy, even in stressful situations, we must change our perspectives and thought patterns. By speaking to your subconscious, you can awaken your potential to stand firm and display resilience even in difficult times. By thinking positively about what you are currently doing, you will find satisfaction, happiness, and a reason to continue moving forward.

The five whys

The five whys is a self-development technique that challenges you to ask yourself a question and follow it up with the five whys. This allows you to get to the core of your answer and to learn about yourself in the process. What do you want to do? Become a fireman? Why do you want that? To feel like you are helping others? And why do you want that? To get a sense of gratitude?

Suddenly you have shed light on your motivation, and you are more able to go after the things you want.

| 5 |

A Growth Mindset

A mindset is a way of thinking. It is a lens that allows you to see what you want in this world. Unlike beliefs and values, a mindset is something that is fairly easy to change with awareness, practice and determination. It is the general perspective you have on life and how you react to various situations. In some ways, you can say that values are what unites us, beliefs can divide us and mindsets will decide if you live a fulfilling and abundant life.

Our mindset can stop us from achieving our goals and accessing our desires in life. It doesn't matter what beliefs or values you have; if you have the wrong mindset, it can limit you and hinder your general sense of happiness. On the other hand, feeding the right mindset will be essential for you to create the life you want.

An individual can have a mindset, but we can also observe mindsets in organisations, groups, families and friends. In the case of a group mindset, it is basically the way that a group will think when together. For example, you might think in more creative ways when you are at work because your team encourages you to think outside the box. The goal is to empower you to switch your mindset to one that will positively transform your life and attract abundance and wealth.

We all have goals and aims, and we all have an idea of what we would like our lives to be like. Despite this though, many of us fail to reach those goals or to actualise our dreams. Why is this? Or to put it another way, what is it that is holding you back? There is a good chance that you already know what the answer is likely to be.

It is you!

All of us have at some point been responsible for getting in our own way at one point or another. Either because of limiting beliefs or because of poor habits and lack of discipline. If you have a fixed mindset, you will be absorbed with what is missing in your life. In that situation, the mind becomes busy worrying and stops you from accessing what you want from life. A fixed mindset will focus on limitation and manifest obstacles which can seriously limit your success. When you limit yourself with your beliefs and actions, you are not open to receive or recognise the abundance that surrounds you. For a fixed mind, there is never enough. The person wakes up in the morning thinking they did not have enough sleep or won't have enough time to accomplish all the things that can be accomplished that day. No matter what it is, the scarcity mind is set on acknowledging what is not available.

How many times have you decided that you want to make a change in your life by getting into shape, starting a new business, or starting a new job... only to then make no progress in those areas? What possible reason could you have for this? Often it comes down to a lack of belief in yourself. It comes down to limiting beliefs about who you are, what you are worth... even how you are meant to behave.

Limiting beliefs are incredibly destructive, largely because we often do not even realise that they are affecting us. They sit quietly in our unconscious brains and gradually prevent us from reaching our full potential. And more importantly, they make us unhappy. They give us a sense of pessimism, which can colour everything we do in negative shades.

These beliefs act as your reference point. They inform every decision and opinion you make. They form your "internal operating system." In other words, every feeling, thought, and experience you have will effectively flow from these beliefs. If you do not replace them with positive ones, you will not get the most out of life – or enjoy it even if you do.

The good news is that we can change our beliefs.

Our very thoughts are capable of changing the structure of our DNA! This incredible fact means that it is entirely possible to transform the way you think… to reset that operating system as it were – and to thereby live a happier and more fulfilled life.

What are limiting beliefs?

I am going to start out by providing a few examples of limiting beliefs:

You cannot start your own business

Let's say that you have a business idea. You are going to provide coaching for small businesses and help them get up and started. You will charge a relatively low flat fee, but then the company will pay you a slightly larger fee a year later as long as their earnings have passed a certain threshold. Your model involves selling directly to the customer, and the way you plan to do this is by looking for them on Instagram. You will find people who post about a business plan, then you will private message them and simply start chatting. If you spot an opportunity to sell, you will pounce. That is the "soft sell" approach, and it means you can build a relationship and demonstrate your value before you charge. Here is the problem though: you are too scared to contact anyone! Every day you put off messaging your clients out of the blue, and you cannot quite put your finger on why.

Chances are it comes down to some limiting beliefs:

- You do not believe anyone would pay for your business idea
- You are worried that if you fail, you will lose something that has been keeping you motivated
- You are a "shy person" and do not like to disturb people

Three limiting beliefs holding you back from capitalising on your dreams.

You will not leave your job/relationship

Let's try another situation. Let's say you are in a job or a relationship that makes you unhappy. It really doesn't matter which, but you know it will not provide you with fulfilment. But you stay there anyway! Why? Because you feel it is the "best you are going to get." A lack of self-esteem means you do not think you can get "better." You effectively think you are not "worth" more than that. And this then leads you to make some terrible mistakes. Some people will even stay in abusive relationships because they do not feel they will find anything better! Some even feel they deserve the abuse they receive.

You throw away the novel you wrote

Did you know that when Stephen King first wrote Carrie, he threw it in the bin? It was his wife who retrieved it for him and told him he was being crazy! It turns out that we often cannot recognise our own talent – or we are too scared to believe in it! Now compare this to someone like J.K. Rowling who persistently kept sending out her manuscript for Harry Potter despite it being rejected over and over! Imagine if Rowling had King's lack of self-belief!

It is something you have always done

Not all limiting beliefs can seem like negative things on the face of it. For example, how about your sense of "self." We all have a sense of who we are, but most of us do not think of this as a limiting belief! Of course, who you think you are is not always limiting… but it can be! A perfect example of this is what happens when you get stuck in "type thinking." This is when you think that you are a certain "type" of person or that you have a certain set of traits… and then you let that dictate who you are going forward.

For example, you might have a reputation for being the class clown. As a result, you always cause a ruckus in the office and draw attention to yourself. Eventually, this starts to hurt your career, but you feel as though you cannot change that about yourself – as it is something you are known for and an integral part of your personality!

As you can see, limiting beliefs really can be extremely problematic and hurt every aspect of your life – and we have still only touched on a few. For this reason, it is time to start doing something about them.

Change your thoughts

What many people do not realise is that they can actually become luckier by changing their beliefs about themselves and what will happen in their lives. This sounds absurd, but it makes a lot of sense once you understand the logic behind it all.

People tend to think that luck is something that is out of their control. After all, that is pretty much the definition of luck; luck is good things happening to you often that you did not directly cause. Luck is winning the lottery, luck is finding a tenner on the floor and luck is being in the right place at the right time and meeting the person who becomes the love of your life/offers you that amazing job.

But while luck might seem out of our hands, we all know some people who just seem to have 'all the luck'. These are the people who have all the good things happen to them and almost seem to have a charmed life... And for one person to be that consistently lucky? It seems a little statistically improbable!

So, what is really going on here?

It all begins with changing your self-perception and your attitude. And you have already taken the first step by reading this book!

The Law of Attraction

You may have heard of the 'law of attraction'. This is the idea that what you put out into the world ultimately dictates what you get back; that as you act, so you will become. Again, this might sound like nonsense – but stop and think about how this might work.

Acting like someone who is very successful might mean dressing smarter, acting more assertive and confident, taking on more responsibility and even walking taller. If you genuinely believe you are successful or destined for success, you will exude this certainty in everything you do. As a result, you will give off a number of signs that tell people you are successful and confident. They will see you in your smart suit, and they will think 'there's a successful and capable person'. And do you know what? They will be more likely to offer you more work, give you promotions and generally help you to succeed as a result. You may have heard the expression 'dress for the job you want'. Actually, you shouldn't just be dressing like a pro; you should be taking on that whole personality in every way that you can so that you give off that aura of success and confidence.

The law of attraction also works in other ways too. Did you know that people who have nicer things often get better Christmas presents? That is because people know their gifts need to be special to stand out and deserve a place in their homes. You should give people with less the better presents because they would appreciate them more, but that is not how life works. Nice things attract more nice things. This is the law of attraction.

The bottom line is that if you do not believe you are capable of greatness, then you likely will not act as though you are. And if you do not act as though you are... you will not be! Hang your head feeling shy and vulnerable, and that is how people will perceive you and therefore treat *you*. Be scared of everything, and you will not take chances that could end up improving your life for the better. But be bold, proud, and powerful, and you can achieve amazing things and transform the way others see you. You can, of course, "fake it until you make it" but it will be much better to read on and see how to actually change your very beliefs from the inside out. To give yourself a growth mindset.

What is a growth mindset?

The opposite of the limiting belief, or fixed mindset, is the growth, or abundance, mindset. With that mindset, we realise that there is enough in this world for everyone to receive. You let go of negative feelings like jealousy, envy or pity for yourself and take matters into your own hands. You move from being a victim in your life to a leader. In addition, you do not focus on the limitation, but you recognise the good things that are already present in your life and set your intention to manifest more of what you want. With a growth mindset, you get up thinking that you will make time to rest in the afternoon and then make a list of what can be accomplished in the day. It is about what is possible or about what is available in the present moment.

A growth mindset describes a set of beliefs and behaviours that allow people to increase their likelihood of success and achieving their goals by making them seek opportunities to learn, gain new skills, improve existing skills, become more resilient and enhance their character and willpower. A growth mindset focuses on the journey of giving things a go and failing until you succeed by viewing life events as opportunities to grown. With a growth mindset you take charge of your success and also of the process of attaining and maintaining it.

Your mindset is what will likely determine how you experience your life and if you enjoy it or not. The benefits of having a growth mindset are endless. Individuals with a growth mindset are, in general, more successful and feel less stress in their daily life. Here are a few other benefits:

- **Appreciate your life:** Individuals who have a growth mindset will appreciate more what they have and also the people in their life.
- **Access more opportunities:** With a growth mindset, more opportunities are revealed because you look for them.
- **Decrease your daily stress:** Because people with a growth mindset are less likely to have expectations that cannot be met, this allows them to live a life that has less stress and disappointment.
- **Reduce your anxiety:** When you strongly believe that there are enough resources for everyone, you automatically trust that you can access what you need when you need it. Instead of finding yourself worrying about what you do not have, you are able

to reduce your anxiety by knowing that you can manifest what you want when you need it.
- **Take control of your life:** When you live with a fixed mindset, you are often living as a victim. Like life happens to you as opposed to you making life happen. An abundance mindset will place you in the driver's seat and give you more control over your life and a greater ability to create what you want to experience.
- **Foster happier and more fulfilling relationships:** We tend to attract people that think like us. If you are stuck in a fixed mindset, you will have the tendency to attract people that limit themselves. Alternatively, if you cultivate a growth mindset, you will start manifesting relationships that are uplifting, supportive and, most of all, that brings more abundance in your life.
- **Improve your health:** People who demonstrate an abundance mindset are more grateful which is tied to better physical and psychological health. They are less likely to experience depression, anxiety, stress, and other chronic disorders that are often connected to one's lifestyle.

As we saw above, a limiting belief, or fixed mindset, sees setbacks as hard to overcome and views things as permanent and unchangeable. Limiting beliefs are where your judgements are not based on facts but your own view of reality.

Now that you know how your beliefs shape your future, the next step is to decide what you need to change. Moving towards a growth mindset starts from a place of self-awareness, where you are able to identify when your mindset is fixed. In a perfect world, you would replace all negative beliefs and reset yourself to be happier and more content. In reality, this is work that takes time – so it makes sense to focus on areas that need the most improvement. What is your priority? A better job? A better relationship? More confidence?

Identifying your limiting beliefs

Another thing to do is to look into your past. So far, of all the things you have achieved and of all the experiences you have had, which means the most to you? By looking at what brought you fulfilment in the past, you can learn about what might bring you fulfilment in the future… Once you have gone through these exercises and seen the things you want for yourself, the next question is: why are you not there yet?

As we have seen already, the answer is almost definitely down to your own beliefs about yourself and about the world. So now you know what you want to accomplish, you can home in on the beliefs you need to change.

Letting go

Learning to let go is a very difficult skill to develop, but it is also one of the most valuable and important if you really want to "reset" your mind and attack life with new positivity and determination. The unfortunate truth is that many of us are defined by our past experiences, and we allow them to colour and guide our future behaviours and judgements.

If you have had a traumatic experience in your past, then this can stay with you and cause you to feel as though you might have further bad luck in future. We often do not give ourselves fully to relationships because of bad relationships we have had in the past, and likewise, old experiences with parents and schoolfriends can shape the way we see ourselves.

If you are to move on with a positive mindset, you need to clear the emotional baggage first. This is something we will all have to go through at one time or another. While you should not try to bury or ignore painful emotions, it is important to embrace them and move on so that you can get on with your life. Wallowing in despair and feeling upset is not a constructive response to any situation and ultimately it will of course result in your failing to build new attachments and to move on with your life. Let us look at some ways you can move on and overcome emotions that potentially might be limiting you and preventing you from getting on with your life.

Get stuck in

Letting go of people and relationships is very different from letting go of projects and ideas. If you have lost a thing, lost a lot of money, or lost your work on a new novel for instance then there is no real emotional aspect to deal with in the same way as there is for a relationship and it is not going to help you at all to spend time wallowing in your upset. As such then, the best solution is to simply move on and focus instead on restarting from scratch. And the best way to do that? That is to simply pick up the pieces and get on with a plan to rebuild. The sooner you rebuild, the less you have lost.

Have a send-off

Whatever it is that you have lost, it is important to deal with those emotions and to get closure. This is why a funeral and a wake are so important following the death of a loved one as they allow us to say goodbye and close that chapter in our lives. You can have a send-off for anything though, whether it is someone you loved or your business. You can even have a celebration to mark the "end" of an influential time in your life, or even to the "old you." This can be a very good way to get rid of the "type thinking" that we already discussed.

Realise the value

The expression "it is better to have loved and lost than never to have loved at all" might not seem comforting to those who have done the former, but it is actually very true. Whether or not the person, relationship or possession is gone, you will have learned and grown from the experience.

The empty chair

Sometimes part of the difficulty with letting go of a loved one or a relationship is that you still have unresolved issues that you haven't had a chance to overcome, and sometimes things go unsaid until it is too late. To help you to move on it is often useful to get these issues off your chest by talking to a chair that you imagine they are sitting on. Another very useful one is to write a letter to them that you then destroy afterwards.

Your automatic memory

You have removed many of the negative lingering emotions and beliefs that come from your old experiences. But what about those that are still there, floating just under the surface? Many of us fall into old patterns and habits based on old experiences but are unaware of them at the time! This is your automatic memory. Essentially your automatic memory is what happens when you do not remember that you remember something.

Usually, when we think of memory, we are describing what is known as "explicit memory." These are the things we can actively recall happening, the things we can relive, and the knowledge we know we have. This is a memory that we access consciously. In the case of automatic memory, though, we are remembering things but are unable to identify what those are. Studies have shown that even when we cannot remember something that happened consciously, it can still end up affecting our behaviour, which seems to demonstrate that we do still remember it in some sense of the word. Even if we do not remember it consciously, there is some kind of "record" of it which can end up impacting us in a number of ways.

An example of automatic memory might be a repressed memory as described by Freud. Here the theory is that highly traumatic memories can be "repressed" to keep them hidden from us consciously because they are too potentially damaging. Mostly, though, this is not the type of automatic memory that is causing limiting beliefs.

Automatic memory is normally evidenced by the existence of "priming" where the participant has no knowledge of such priming. Priming occurs when we are subject to certain experiences and scenarios that might alter our perception or our behaviour. For instance, you can prime yourself to be more aggressive by spending time watching lots of aggressive films in a hot room with red walls. Similarly, you could prime yourself to respond to questions in a certain way to make yourself more likely to answer subsequent questions using the same reference.

Automatic memory could also be used to describe other "types" of memory, such as muscle memory, that do not have a semantic element to them for us to remember consciously. A knee-jerk reaction, for instance, could result from an experience, even though we might not remember that event or link the two. Procedural memories allow us to do such things as writing or riding a bike, or reading, though again, they do not tend to require conscious "remembering." The reason this is relevant and interesting to us is that it shows us once again just how our actions are shaped by forces we are not even aware of. And this becomes particularly problematic when you find yourself constantly thinking things like, "I am going to fail." While you might not realise it, those implicit memories are actually influencing your subsequent decisions and your beliefs generally.

The illusion of truth is an example of a cognitive bias that may be related to the concept of implicit memory. Essentially the "illusion of truth effect" says that we are more likely to believe a statement to be true if we have heard it before, even if we do not remember having heard it. The reason is that we think "that sounds familiar", or it registers on some unconscious level, and thus we conclude that there must be truth to it. This effect occurs without the need for conscious acknowledgement of the memory, which demonstrates the role of automatic memory.

While the subject of automatic memory is a relatively new one, there is enough evidence for automatic memory affecting decision-making through priming and other mechanisms to warrant consideration. This is a topic that self-help books have been quick to jump on – without always fully understanding the concept. Nevertheless, it is possible that some of your behaviours and feelings may be affected by memories that you are not aware of.

It has been suggested by some that this could explain why we sometimes find ourselves in bad moods or feeling anxious without knowing why. It could be that something we have encountered has triggered an association and an emotional response, even though we may not remember that association forming in the first place. It is also worth bearing in mind that it can cause us to make unwise decisions or to believe things that are not necessarily true. If you feel like something must be true because it sounds familiar, or you feel drawn to a particular course of action without knowing why then try taking a moment to really assess your emotions and where they are coming from before you let them completely dictate your actions.

So what are we going to take away from this? One powerful tip is to think about all those things that are shaping your emotions and thoughts without you even being aware of them. Think about your environment and the thoughts and beliefs you tell yourself regularly.

Positive affirmations

You can influence these things positively, on the other hand, by using "positive affirmations." Try placing cards around your home that tell you positive things or remind you of positive times. And find a handful of positive affirmations that resonate with you. Say these to yourself a number of times each day, and you will eventually find yourself exuding positivity.

Moods

And when you find yourself in a bad mood or about to make a pessimistic determination – ask yourself where this might be coming from. Could it be something that has been affecting you unconsciously? Just knowing that our feelings and thoughts can come from "outside" will often do a lot to help us get them back under control.

Positive CBT

Many of the techniques we have looked at so far in this book have a lot in common with cognitive behavioural therapy. CBT is the psychotherapeutic approach that involves changing the way you think through a two-part process: assessing current thoughts and replacing them with positive ones. The most potent part of this mix is something called "cognitive restructuring." This tool can be used to destroy damaging beliefs that might be leading to self-destructive behaviour.

Mindfulness

One aspect of cognitive restructuring is mindfulness, which, as we have already seen, simply means paying more attention to the contents of your own thoughts. The idea is to listen to the thoughts you are having without influencing them - watching them "go by like clouds" so that you can then identify the negative ones you are having. You need to learn to spot these negative thoughts when they crop up, and then use reframing to replace them.

Reframing negative thoughts

Reframing your negative thought when you spot them means finding a positive alternative to replace the negative thought you had. Typical examples would be:

INSTEAD OF	SAY
I do not know how to do this	I will learn how to do this
I am no good at it	I am in the process of learning it
I have made too many mistakes	Mistakes are how I learn and get better
Everyone is so far ahead of me	I am proud of where I am in the journey, and inspired by those ahead of me
I am not good enough	I am enough, I have enough
I will never be successful	I am in the right place, at the right time, doing the right thing

I do not have enough money	I am resilient in the face of challenges
It is too complicated	I will tackle it from a different angle

This is why the affirmations discussed earlier in this book are so powerful. But there are two more useful methods in cognitive restructuring too. One is "thought challenging", and the other is "hypothesis testing." In thought challenging, you look at the content of the negative ruminations and then really ask yourself whether they are accurate. Your job here is to truthfully deconstruct your negative beliefs and to prove yourself wrong about them in a way that is impossible to argue. So, if you think that "nobody cares what happens to me" and that is a reason for destructive behaviour, you would assess if this is really true.

Ask yourself: if something happened to you, is it really true that nobody would care? Is there not one person who would be horrified to lose you? And do you not owe it to them to look after yourself? As you can see, thought challenging will reveal many of the thoughts you tell yourself to, in fact, be thinly veiled deceptions. Hypothesis testing takes this to the next level by getting you to test the theory – to see if your assertion is true. This is only appropriate in certain circumstances of course.

You can likewise use thought challenging to crush fears about starting a new business or about spending time with friends (hypothesis testing is also great for this one) and you can use mindfulness in every aspect of your life to better understand your own beliefs and motivations.

Self-esteem

Low self-esteem is a problem that can end up affecting countless other areas of your life. It is one of the biggest limiting beliefs of them all. In itself, low self-esteem can be highly detrimental to your mood on a daily basis and to your enjoyment of any activities you participate in. On top of that, low self-esteem also means you make less of an impression on the people you meet, you are less likely to take chances (the good kind) and you are more likely to experience mental health problems like depression.

In short, if this is something you struggle with, it is crucial to start working to improve your sense of self-worth so that you can get more out of life and prevent a potential downward spiral.

But how do you do that? There are countless articles and pieces of advice out there but many of them fail to really address the issues leading to low self-esteem or the severity of the problem. A lot of articles for instance will tell you to "take care of your personal hygiene" – as though cleaning your teeth a minute longer is going to magically fix your lack of self-worth. As much as it might be nice to simply will yourself into having more esteem or to make lists of things you love about yourself, that is not going to cure a deeply ingrained crisis in confidence.

Something we may think of as being responsible for low self-esteem is the "dorsolateral prefrontal cortex" which serves as – among other things – our "inner critic." When this goes into overdrive, we question everything, and it is this questioning and doubting that can lead to low confidence and low self-esteem. In fact, confidence can pretty much be defined as "not questioning your decisions or statements."

Being able to turn off the dorsolateral prefrontal cortex when in social settings can immediately mitigate the effects of low self-esteem by allowing you to be more "in the moment." In turn, this will make you more fluent, and you will come away having had positive social experiences that can help with combating anxiety.

How do you shut down your inner critic? One method is meditation which can teach you the mental discipline to stay in the here and now. Otherwise, just try to focus on whatever you are doing and react in the moment. Stop thinking about what you are going to say and listen. The more you focus and engage with what you are doing, the more the DLPC switches off.

This is one of the reasons that meditation is such a powerful tool for helping to combat negative feelings and beliefs and getting you to feel more positive and optimistic.

Another tip? Do things you are truly passionate about to smash apart those negative beliefs and feelings!

The way you use positive CBT in the context of self-esteem is to look at the content of the "inner critic" and to see what it is that you are telling yourself that is making you feel low. Your job is then to change this inner script while at the same testing those theories and proving to yourself that they are not true. Think you are too shy or uninteresting? Prove yourself wrong by putting yourself in uncomfortable situations. Cognitive behavioural therapists will encourage you to do this, but you now know one of the best ways, which is to constantly be "hypothesis testing", as discussed previously. Put yourself in a demanding job that is just outside your comfort zone, and that requires lots of interactions. As you find yourself rising to meet challenges, you will give that inner critic less and less "ammunition" against you, and your confidence will rise rapidly!

Body language

Understanding automatic memory has shown us how something that we are not even consciously aware of can end up "priming" our mood and making us more positive or less so. One of the biggest ways you can do this? Change the way you look, the way you stand... and even your expression! This affects the way we feel about ourselves on a very deep and impactful level.

One way to help others to think you are more confident is to change your body language subtly. Placing one arm on a door frame can help you to look as though you believe you own the space. Likewise, spreading out more, in general, suggests more dominance and confidence.

Being still and calm also exudes confidence and makes you look like you are cool and in command. The aim is not to be aggressive but to recognise when you are doing the opposite (curling into a ball and generally shrinking) and to cut out those behaviours. And next time you walk into a room, puff your chest up as you enter the door and "beam."

What is more, the right body language can even drive the production of feel-good hormones and neurotransmitters that make you more confident. Standing in a victory pose (arms in a V shape) in the bathroom before an interview can elevate testosterone and help you to be more effective in that interview!

We all think of smiling as a good thing and something we should do more, and we realise the benefits it can have on our popularity and on the moods of the people around us. However, what we maybe do not realise is what it can do for the other areas of our lives – how simply smiling can actually make everything a lot better and even advance our careers. First of all, thanks to something called "facial feedback', simply smiling can be one of the very best ways to improve your mood. Simply by smiling it is possible to improve your mood as it causes your body to release more positive hormones – in fact, any expression that you pull has been shown to have this facial feedback effect. Next time you are feeling lethargic and tired then, simply try smiling, and you will find it improves your mood to no end.

At the same time, because you are producing positive hormones and endorphins, rather than damaging ones like cortisones, this can then have a strengthening effect on your immune system and generally help you to become more resilient against illnesses and other problems. Of course, it can also help with motivation and psychological well-being no end.

If you thought that facial feedback was an impressive effect, you will likely be more impressed still with the "mirror neurons" in our brain, which fire when we see someone else pull an expression too. This means that the expression you see someone else pull can also cause you to produce the respective hormones and alter your mood. It means that when you smile at someone, it automatically causes them to produce endorphins and to feel happier too. If you smile every time you see someone, they will feel happier every time they see you too. This in turn then means that you can essentially create an association where they see you and then think of feeling happy and good about themselves. This association will then ensure that they are more likely to want to spend time with you and that will boost your social life, aid your career and help you to become more likely to succeed generally.

At the same time, because you look happier and more confident, this will also lead people to believe that you are both of those things. And when you seem more confident and happier, people tend to assume you are more successful (which would be the reason you are feeling confident) which in turn ensures that they think you are more likely to be highly capable. This can help you in relationships and certainly in your career, as you have an aura around you of someone who is successful and whom you would want on your side.

As you can see, changing the way you look and act can make you become the person you want.

Do not just dress for the job you want… dress for the life you want!

Meditation and the growth mindset

Meditation is something that is often misunderstood. Many people think it is somehow mystical or unscientific. In fact, meditation is simply a term describing a range of different practices, each with a single purpose and effect: to train and exercise focus. The meditation many people know of is transcendental meditation. Here, practitioners sit in the lotus position and focus on a single "mantra", such as a hum or a word. The result? You completely clear your mind and thus learn to rise "above" the many petty concerns that previously made you stressed and unhappy.

Likewise, religious meditation means doing the same thing – focusing on a passage of religious text or a prayer.

In tai chi (moving meditation), the focus is on the body. However you do it, the main objective is to direct the mind and to avoid letting thoughts and feelings bog you down.

Mindfulness can also be practised as a form of meditation. Here, you do not try to empty your mind but just focus on the contents of your thoughts, without letting them affect you. This is useful for CBT and cognitive restructuring, as described earlier. But all types of meditation have one more powerful effect: they help you to decide what to focus on and how to feel.

That means that the next time you find yourself feeling completely overwhelmed, you can simply decide to ignore the negative voice in your ear and to focus instead on the positive. All the other changes we have made in this book become far more powerful once you gain control of your focus and your thoughts. When we direct our attention, we tell our brains what is important, and what is accurate. As a result, we are able to trigger physical alterations in our brains, that can eliminate negative, limiting beliefs and help to make us into smarter, happier, and more confident versions of ourselves!

| 6 |

Success

Everyone wants success but is it for everyone? People will tell you that anyone can be successful at anything they want only if they put their mind to it. But is that how success works? Is it really that simple?

Not exactly!

If anything, success comes at a cost. Most people don't become successful because they are not willing to pay the price of success. It is a choice they must make where they must step out of the box, make some changes to their existing lifestyle, drop old habits and pick up new ones and invest effort, attitude and morale to keep things going.

But if you are willing to learn and transform yourself in all the right areas, then success is definitely for you. If you are going to set yourself up for success in life, then you need to set some meaningful goals. As a starting point, the first and foremost thing to remember on the journey of personal success is a positive attitude towards everything.

If you fail once, get back up and prove yourself instead of bringing yourself down with negativity. Tell yourself through every obstacle and hardship, 'I did not come this far, to ONLY come this far'. No success is achieved overnight, no mountain is climbed without a few falls. If others can put up a fight to achieve personal success despite countless hardships, so can you.

Aiming high

It is always better to aim high, even if you do not succeed at first. When you aim big, you dream big, and tell yourself that you stand a chance against all odds. The problem with setting lower standards is that the lower you set your aim, the more you limit yourself. You miss more chances, and more of your abilities are left unexplored.

It is your own personal belief, unwavering resilience and ambitions that will lead you to achieve your ultimate dream. But the moment you start to doubt yourself, the moment you decide you cannot aim higher for fear of failure, is when your downfall begins. With a higher aim, you may miss at first, or you may make it on your first try. the higher your aim, the more you achieve. Even if you fall short of your goal, you won't end up too far from it. Just think of achieving a good score on a test. If you aim low at getting a 50% mark on the test, you might be successful and achieve that. But that is all it will be; an average and low achievement. If you aim higher at getting 90%, you may miss and hit 80%, which is still higher and so much better than the low set aim of 50%. The same goes for all tests and trials life puts you through.

Set goals that align with your purpose

When setting goals, you need to think about how to achieve them, what you need to do to achieve them, and how much time you need to get there. Why is it a priority? Why is it so important?

Setting goals is easy. Just think of drawing up a New Year's resolution. Everyone does that every year. So much so that it becomes a mere habit and not much else. But what people do not is pause to think over the goal and question, "Why?" Without this driving force, they lose motivation and fail to achieve their goal. As such, it is important to not merely set goals but to set purpose-driven goals instead. For example, you may be thinking of hitting the gym, working out and getting yourself in shape. With just this in mind, you set a goal in your New Year's resolution to work out every day. You do it the first day and the second, and something comes up on the third. Then you end up skipping the fourth day because you lose the momentum and get lazier. In the end, you achieve nothing and set the same goal for next year's resolution.

On the other hand, an obese person on the verge of getting diabetes and a possible heart attack is told by the doctor he needs to work out and lose weight really soon if he still wants a chance at a healthy life, or maybe just life. This is his 'Why'. This is why he won't skip the third or fourth day, no matter what comes up. This is why he will achieve his goal with more determination.

Set a timeframe

Without setting a timeframe to achieve any particular goal, there will be no sense of urgency. The importance of getting anything done is great, but the importance of getting it done in time is even greater! Giving yourself a duration for a specific task will make you more productive in that short time than you would be without it. If you know the deadline for a task is 24 hours, you will make yourself attend to that task as a priority. You will utilise those 24 hours in the most effective way possible to complete the task at hand. If you set a deadline of one week for the same task, not only will you waste the entire week and be less productive, but you will also waste precious time that you could have used to complete other tasks as well.

Having said that, the timeframe has to be realistic and attainable. You need to be sure whether the goal is a short-term goal or a long-term one. Losing 10 kg in 3 days? Not possible, not attainable, even if you spend most of the hours of the three days in the gym. The timeframe should not be based on some delusion. An understanding of the goal and the priority you are willing to give it can help you decide better how much time you will allocate each day to get it done.

If you have an essay due next week, and you keep delaying it or doing it in bits, paragraph by paragraph a day, it will get tiresome and boring. In the end, it might not even make a lot of sense. Plus, you will lose the sense of urgency that could make you more productive. But if you decide to do it in two days, you will utilise those two days much more effectively and will even have time for other goals once you finish that essay. The less you linger on with the task at hand, the better.

Decision-making

Everyone has to make decisions in their daily life. While some of them are small, others are big and have a profound impact on your life. So, it is very important to evaluate all aspects of an issue before coming to a decision. There are a few things that, if considered, can help you make better decisions:

Do it!

People are always making decisions about the changes they want to bring in life but often end up ignoring them. You must carry out your decision. If you have strong willpower and are dedicated to something, you will be able to carry it out. For example, if you decide to join a book club in your local library, push yourself to do it as soon as possible. When you delay something, the chances of it never happening increase. Schedule a day to visit the library today and accomplish your task on that given day, no matter what. A very common example in this regard is smokers. There are so many people out there who want to quit smoking. They have researched everything, and they have planned everything out, but they fail to carry out their decision. If you keep postponing it, you will never be able to achieve it.

Why start tomorrow when you can do it today? You can quit smoking if you put your heart and mind to it. There are so many others who have done it. Read the stories of people online or join a help group so that you have the motivation you need. Interacting with people who have succeeded in carrying out their decisions will help you immensely.

Do not give up if you fail the first time. Learn from the mistakes you made on the first attempt. Ask yourself how you can succeed the next time. Remember that you can do it. Nothing or no one can stop you if you put your mind to something. Learn from your past mistakes and act on them until it is done.

The first step

It is the first step that counts the most. Most people put off their important tasks to 'Tomorrow', 'Next Week' or even 'Next Year'. In their mind, they even subconsciously tell themselves that they are not ready. But the truth to the matter is we can never be 100% ready. In other words, they procrastinate. Remember that there is never a better time to start than now. Just take that first step, and the road will lead on.

Do not look back

It is not always easy to carry out your decisions. There will most likely be hurdles along the way. If you want to quit smoking, you might be peer-pressured to derail from this decision. Or people around you could tell you that one smoke a day doesn't do any harm. You need to remember why you started in the first place. Before you made this decision, you must have thought a lot about the health and social changes it will bring to your life. Every time you feel like you are derailing from your path, remember why you started the journey in the first place.

You might even have to cut off things and people to carry out your decisions. Cut out people from your life who pressure you into smoking. It might be hard at first, but you need to remember that these people are toxic to you. If someone is bringing negativity into your life, why keep them close?

Do not let apathy or lack of a proper schedule derail you from this decision. Do not let your apathy stop you from doing things that are good for you. Sometimes, you make mistakes when you carry out a decision. Do not let that stop you from continuing. Make proper plans and stick to them. Start making decisions and carry them out without stopping for anyone or anything. You will be thankful to yourself for the positive impact these decisions have on your life.

Consistency

Consistency is the magic ingredient for success, be it personal betterment, business, academics or just the relationships with loved ones. Without consistency and the will to stay resolute in what you are trying to achieve, only failure awaits. A child can never tie his shoelaces on the very first try, he will only succeed when he tries again over and over until he finally figures it out the hundredth time. The same goes for adults, do you think anyone can play the piano flawlessly on their first attempt? The important thing is not to do it once but to do it over and over again. Never stop until you achieve total mastery.

Commitment and perseverance

Perseverance means having unwavering persistence in accomplishing anything no matter the difficulties and obstacles along the way. With perseverance, you can learn new skills, pass exams, close a deal, and achieve financial and personal success. Just like solving a jigsaw puzzle, if the piece doesn't fit, try another one, and then another one until it is completed. Without it, the puzzle would be left incomplete. Similarly, all goals are left unachieved, all success is unknown until we learn to stay committed and persevere.

Push yourself to be patient and stay committed. Tell yourself why it is important that you stay committed, and remind yourself of why you must go on. Anyone can try once and give up, but only those who stay committed and persevere succeed in life. In being persistent towards achieving any goal in life, you learn from your failures. You learn what went wrong the first time. You learn how to overcome these obstacles rather than being paralysed by them. Everything in life demands this commitment, from a successful career to a healthy relationship.

Set a routine

Having a routine is vital for success in general. Without the proper allotment of time you give to a particular task every day, there is no way of achieving consistency. It should be such that your mind automatically rings a bell to remind you what you must be doing at that particular hour. Without a routine, a change in the timing of one thing would lead to a change in the other.

So everything needs a proper allocation of time. What time do you wake up? How long do you work out for? What time do you eat? How much time can you afford to give to your hobbies? Are you giving enough time to friends and family? All this needs to be set in order to achieve success. Being consistent with a routine maximises the benefits of all the hard work. In the long term, having a messed-up routine will not only stand in your way of success but also mess up other aspects of life as well.

Good habits

Being consistent leads to the development of good habits. Creating good habits ensures success in all areas of life. Doing something once in a while or when you get the time doesn't get you anywhere near achieving your aims and aspirations. Instead, the keys to achieving any goals you set are consistency and making quick decisions. This decision to do something every day is, in other words, your habits.

The first thing to keep in mind for creating good habits is to choose discipline and your priority over your mood. 'I'm not in the mood to study today, might as well binge-watch a series'. 'I'm a bit too upset to work out today; skipping one day should not hurt.' We have all been there. We have all chosen the 'mood' over consistency, which has eventually led to a failure in developing good habits. To help you stick to the good habits you create, it is a good idea to track your progress. This helps you know how beneficial the habit has been for you. The clearer you see the results, the more motivated you will be to persist until you succeed.

For example, if you have a goal set on your weight and how much you want to lose, keeping a record every week should help you see a clearer pattern of the good that is coming from your habit of exercise. When you see the actual figure on the scale, you will get more enthusiastic and positive about your workout and how it turns out for you. No results can be seen overnight. Nothing is achieved in one go. Achievements require a long, persistent struggle. Success is not out of reach, it is only difficult to reach. Through persistence, perseverance and commitment, success can be guaranteed. Consistency leads to the development of good habits; good habits lead to actions, and that gets all the work done. Once you get used to the struggles and stay committed no matter what the difficulties are, no failures can set you back. They can only make you stronger and more ambitious than ever to reach your goals.

Be positive

Everyone says that nothing is impossible. But do they actually believe it? If you really want everything to be possible, you have to start believing it. You would be surprised by the power that belief has in life. You can make everything possible if you condition your mind to think so.

Optimism is an essential part of success in life. Once you condition your mind to think "well and good", it will have a positive impact on all your decisions and thoughts. Having a positive outlook on life is the first step to achieving success. You will never become a brilliant photographer if you keep telling yourself that it is impossible for you to capture something beautiful. What do you need to do instead? You need to be positive and think positively. Keep telling yourself that you can do it. But do not just say it; you must mean it and feel the emotions coursing through your veins like it is real! As a human being, you will feel pessimistic from time to time. Do not fight it; embrace that thought, take a deep breath and ask yourself: Is this thought or emotion empowering me or disempowering me? Practice this daily, and eventually, you will find yourself more inclined to have positive thoughts rather than negative ones.

People like J. K. Rowling failed in their first attempts too. Did they give up? No. instead, they kept their minds positive and kept striving. Now, one of them is the creator of a literary masterpiece. If they told themselves that it is impossible for them to achieve something just because they failed the first time, would they have succeeded? Never.

Attitude

Your attitude matters a lot. If you are not serious about something, you cannot expect to excel at it. So, you have made up your mind about learning to play the piano. To learn, you must stay determined.

There must be no going back once you have made up your mind. Keep reminding yourself that you are only stopping once you have made it possible. Do not be apathetic about something. If you have joined a piano class for learning, go to it regularly. Do not miss a class just because you do not feel like going or you are too lazy to go. Tell yourself that missing even one day will put you behind.

But bear in mind that it is crucial not to listen to others blindly. People like to share their experiences, especially when they have failed in the past. Someone might tell you that you will never learn because they themselves did not manage to. If someone failed at something, that does not mean you will too. Maybe they did not have the dedication or positive outlook. But as long as you possess positivity and determination, you will succeed.

Most importantly, have faith in yourself. When you wake up every day, tell yourself that it is possible for you to do it. Remind yourself of all the challenges that you have already overcome and prepare for the ones you are going to face. Think of a school or college. Everyone goes to the same place and has the same teachers, books and environment. So why is it that some of them manage to excel at their studies while others do not? They must be doing something extra that others are not. It is their attitude that takes them forward. They work extremely hard and do not let anything stop them from getting what they want.

Accept setbacks

When you start a journey, you are bound to face bumps along the road. You must be prepared for everything.

In the chapter on goal setting, we saw how a Hope Map could help prepare us for these bumps and be prepared to implement the "Plan B" you identified when you did this exercise.

Gratitude

Sometimes, one thing can ruin an entire day or week. Learn to look at the bigger picture and think of all the positive things that happened that day. A good way to do this is to keep a gratitude journal. Write down everything that you are grateful for. Then, every time you are hit with failure or a hurdle, read the journal to feel better. A popular quote teaches us that nothing is impossible because the word itself says that "I'm possible". Keep this in mind every time you face difficulties.

Also, surround yourself with a positive environment and supportive peer groups. Use positive words when you define your life or purpose. Spend time with people who will always push you forward and encourage you rather than telling you to give up after the first blow. When you have learnt how to channel your inner energy and keep your mind positive, you realise that nothing is impossible. It is only impossible until it is done. So, do it and make it possible.

Accountability

There comes a certain time in your life when you realise that you are accountable for everything you do. The idea is quite daunting, as accountability is needed in all spheres of life. The first step to being accountable is to take responsibility. It might be a personal responsibility or one that affects others around you. Remember this: With great power comes great responsibility. Take full responsibility for your actions, and do not make excuses when something goes wrong. You need to realise that you are in charge, and therefore you should be held accountable.

Personal mission statement

Make a mission statement for yourself. Start with revisiting the chapter on Meaning. Your mission statement is a statement that identifies your purpose in life, how you aim to pursue that purpose and how you intend to pursue it. Write it down somewhere so that you can read it every day. One tip is to set your phone's wallpaper with inspirational quotes and positive affirmations so that you can look at them every day and be inspired every time you pick up your phone.

Honesty

Just as accountability is important, so is honesty. It is very important to be honest about the results. Whether you are working alone or in a team, you must stay honest about the outcome of your efforts. Success only becomes possible when you own up to your mistakes. While they can be cumbersome, mistakes are also valuable learning opportunities. If you have done something wrong, own it. Ask yourself why it happened and what you can do to make it right. If you totally ignore it or lie about it to yourself and others, how can you ever hope to rectify it?

Plus, when you are not honest with yourself, you will always have a constant feeling of dissatisfaction. Your conscience will not let you forget it. Be honest about the goals you set. Be realistic. Holding yourself accountable for your actions is also a reality check to set goals that are attainable.

If you think your goals are realistic, proceed with them. A good way to prevent disappointment and failure is to do the pathways in the Hope Map we talked about earlier, even when you are setting realistic goals, because there are always likely to be obstacles along the way. Being accountable can be a frightening thought because no one likes to be judged. But if you follow the right strategy and put in the effort, you will be able to master the art of accountability.

Live in the moment

Living in the moment means being fully aware and mindful of the present moment. It may involve some effort on your part, as it means not dwelling unnecessarily on the past or being overly anxious about the future. To live in the moment is to seize the moment you are in, live it to the fullest, and experience it without letting the past or the future distract you.

In fact, living in the moment means acknowledging that "someday" will never come. If anything, it is already here. It is right now, so do not put off your goals just because it is not the right time or you lack funds. You can still work toward your goals despite these setbacks. The time may never be right unless you are prepared for it. So, prepare right now.

The entire idea of living in the now, and not just 'living' it, means realising the importance of it, giving it the emotions and thoughts that it rightfully demands. Focusing on what you have now, focusing on the task at hand now, and focusing on all that you can thank today for.

Being present in the now and being mindful of the very moment you are living in allows you to make it even more valuable and meaningful. Instead of pondering over the past or worrying over the future, make the most of the present. Make the most out of the opportunity at hand, not letting distractions take away what you have now. Feel the moment and embrace it. Unless you learn to be present and mindful of the moment, you won't be able to give it your best.

Meditation

If you find yourself giving in to distractions easily, consider meditation. Meditation can be very helpful in learning how to live in the moment. It is a practice that helps find inner peace and acceptance, both of which are essential for being mindful of the present moment.

It is also a great way to relax so that you are able to let go of all the stress, anxiety and thoughts of the past or future that haunt you. Unless you are truly relaxed, there is no living in the moment because the present gets overshadowed by the past or the future.

Even breathing during meditation has a significant effect. Deep and relaxing breaths help you feel like you are taking in positive energy and getting rid of negativity burdening your mind. With a couple of deep breaths, you can feel relaxation and inner peace. Take your time and appreciate those moments of peaceful solitude. Making a daily habit of meditation will help you stay calm and focused on the present moments throughout the day.

Constantly letting the past distract you keeps you tied to it, restricting you from making the most of the present. And constantly thinking about the future will not serve you. The past and the future are not in your control. But you control the present moment, so live the moment and make every second count. As the present is what shapes the future. Measuring your success by what you have now is so much more than imagining what it could have been or could be.

Be Adventurous

Being adventurous is to experience something different from the norm, something exciting and maybe even risky. For every individual, the meaning of the word 'adventure' differs greatly. For some, it may just be staying up late, and for others, it could be skydiving, climbing Mount Everest, learning scuba diving, etc.

Being adventurous and challenging yourself is what shapes your character and forms new memories, which makes this life worthwhile. Without adventure, the daily grind of life slowly strips away excitement and experiences that are important for the growth of a person. Adventures contribute to keeping relationships from getting dull.

Your comfort zone

Your comfort zone can be a very small, confined space. In this small space, all things are familiar to you. There are no new experiences, no new lessons to learn and no challenges. Stepping out of your comfort zone means trying new things that you are not comfortable or familiar with. Try doing things you have not done before or never thought you would ever do. Push yourself to get new experiences, to get some excitement in life.

Confining yourself to your comfort zone will never allow you to grow as a person. And it will definitely stand in the way of achieving any success. It does not mean you need to transform everything about yourself. Rather, it is something you need to do for yourself once in a while. You can never enjoy doing the same things over and over. A little adrenaline rush never did any harm. Without stepping out of your comfort zone and being adventurous, you will one day look back at your life and see nothing but a plateau. Adventures and things we do for excitement are the 'highs' in life. The best and most joyful moments can never be experienced in that small, confined place we call a 'comfort zone'.

The fear of the unknown and unfamiliar can make it hard to do so. But once you learn to take little steps out of your comfort zone, you realise how the benefits far outweigh the fears. And only after this will you be able to take big leaps out of your comfort zone and be adventurous. It will help you learn more about yourself and about your strengths and weaknesses.

Open-mindedness

To enrich life with adventures, it is important to be open-minded and to learn from experiences. To be open-minded is to accept that there are things you do not know about and things that you could be wrong about. It means being open to the idea of changing your open-minded thoughts, opinions and perceptions from new experiences and being open to new challenges and ideas.

For example, a narrow-minded person will always respond with a 'no', when asked to join in anything exciting. A pessimist would not only refuse but also go on to explain all the things that could possibly go wrong. An open-minded person, on the other hand, would be open to not only hearing about new ideas but also trying out something new and adventurous. It is the same as one ordering the same thing from the menu every time compared to one trying out new items and cuisines. The latter will have far better experiences, some good and some bad.

Every time you experience something new, there is always a new lesson to be learnt. However, this doesn't mean risking your safety and security for an adventure. It doesn't mean putting your life or the life of others at risk. What it means, instead, is that you need to let yourself out of the shell that makes you feel safe and at ease. To prioritise adventure over convenience means that you are willing to go that extra mile to bring some excitement to your life

Whereas growth leads to learning, creating, doing, resisting and failing; comfort leads to stability, pleasure, protection and safety. But growth cannot happen if you choose comfort over learning. And success means growing, overcoming obstacles, and maybe even failing, but then getting up and trying again. So you cannot continue to keep clinging to the "easy" and avoiding what is "challenging" if you want to be successful.

Language

Words and language are unique to human beings only. They are like power, which you can either use for good or bad. Unfortunately, people do not often realise the impact words can have. Whether it is the expression of love, the instructions in a manual or the speech of a captain just before a game, the words we use can change our outlook on everything.

In fact, words probably linger longer in our memories than actual faces or whole events. So it is wise not to underestimate what words can do for you and others. Has someone ever passed a remark that makes you insecure? Things like "you have a funny smile", and "you have a big nose" scar you with insecurities. That is how words mould your beliefs. It is how words from others change what you think of yourself.

The same goes for compliments. It is surprising how a few words of appreciation can make you believe in yourself. A simple "this colour looks so good on you" will subconsciously always make you look for that colour. Or words of appreciation from a teacher or mentor will encourage you to work harder and improve. This is exactly how words factor into success and failure. A common example of this is what you hear from a doctor. If the doctor speaks kindly and reassures the patient time and again that there is hope and a high chance of recovery, the patient will feel eased and better right away. If the doctor doesn't give any such reassurance and just hands over a prescription, the patient will stay restless and unsure about his or her treatment.

The words you use can pave your way to success or downfall. Speakers make a living out of it. Be it a religious speaker, a motivational speaker, or a teacher. They all use their vocabulary to their best in order to convey things better to you, in order to improve your understanding of a concept and leave an impact on you. When sitting through a job interview, you are basically being assessed on how you speak. The qualifications are all there on the resume, but the ability to communicate only comes through words. A candidate who sounds more convincing and capable has a higher chance of securing the job, even if others are more qualified. The right words are not only more convincing but will also be an indicator of how well-read you are. Even in relationships, the choice of words can either save a relationship or break one. With the right words, you can be more expressive of your feelings (good or bad) so that the other person knows exactly how you feel. It keeps things from getting boring and monotonous. Learn to use other expressions to tell them how you feel, boost their confidence, and give them encouragement.

I can or I can't

These are words that are entirely related to you. They can either make you or break you. Read a new recipe that looks delicious but complicated. Was your answer "I can't do this"? This is your negative self-talk at play again. Do you think that you can succeed in anything if your words betray you from the very beginning? So be aware of your self-talk consciously or subconsciously. What you put behind the word 'I' or 'I am' will impact your beliefs greatly. The more self-defeating words you use, the more opportunities in life you will miss out on.

The ratio of often you use "I can'" or "I can't" can bring much more success and positivity in your life. "I can" will symbolise all the risks you are willing to take, all the new things you are willing to try, all the chances you take, the faith you have in yourself, the limits that you establish for yourself and how much you are willing to push yourself to achieve what you want.

"I can't", on the other hand, symbolises the exact opposite. It is all the chances you missed, the times you refused to see if you could push past an obstacle, the opportunities that you passed by and basically failed without even a single try! Try making your choice of words positive using "I can" so that you can reprogram your subconscious mind to believe things about yourself, your potential, and your aspirations. Because what you believe about yourself can have a real impact on the outcome of events. It is in your own control which of these words you use for yourself.

Learning

Learning is not limited to how many school and college years you have had. Instead, it is a constant, ongoing process of evolution. One that involves acknowledging that you do not know everything. It is an important factor in shaping your personality, introducing new concepts and ideas and helping you educate yourself without any limitations. The worst thing you could do to yourself is to insist that you already know everything.

But choosing to evolve is not always easy. Evolving means mastering success by continuously becoming a better version of your current self. It also implies that you are humble enough to accept correction and improvement.

Improvement

In order to become the best version of yourself, you need to implement this rule in your life. Accept the fact that no information you have is already complete, and there could be more to know about it. Be open to more knowledge and facts instead of being rigid and deciding that what you already know is final and enough. Not being open to constant improvements and knowledge would make you think, 'I've already passed that, I do not need to waste any time reading this'. On the other hand, you can approach new things as a lifelong learner, in which you will learn and gain so much more and improve as an overall human being.

While at school, our parents or teachers made us study and learn whatever was in the curriculum. After that, you were on your own, and learning became a self-motivated task. It is a personal choice you make every day that doesn't necessarily apply to studies alone. Instead, it applies to the overall education you have. You could learn from a documentary that is completely unrelated to your career. You could learn how to milk cows from a relative who owns a farm. Or you could learn how to make jam from your grandmother. The point is just to learn, from anywhere, about anything.

There are so many reasons why you should never stop learning, and not one logical reason why you shouldn't. The struggle and desire to learn all your life can shape your personality for the better. Everyone knows one person in their circle who is charismatic and interesting to talk to. Someone who genuinely has something to contribute to conversations instead of mere opinions. Someone who has knowledge and stories to share with everybody. Such are lifelong learners. When people never stop learning, they also decide to be more independent, useful, and hence, successful. Learning also makes you more influential. It makes people consider your opinion and take whatever you say seriously because you know your stuff based on facts rather than intuition.

The ability to learn and adapt is the key to achieving success in any field. You need to be constantly upgrading your knowledge every day to stay at the top of your chosen field. In your chosen field of commitment, always engage in maintenance learning to keep you on track and stop you from falling behind. If you need to improve your skills, you should get into some growth learning. This type of learning expands the mind by teaching you skills you did not have before.

And finally, there is something called shock learning. For the most part, this can potentially be the most beneficial type of learning as you first have to unlearn something that you already knew before. Here you have to relearn the new information, which gives you new insight into an old situation. Unfortunately, most people choose to ignore this in favour of past information and sabotage their own success. You must never be afraid of change.

Often, we are guilty of not being 'open' to learning new things. If someone tries to correct our facts, we end up getting into an argument because we are too stubborn to admit that we could be wrong and the other person is actually doing us a favour. It is important to remember that the most precious commodity in life is not money but time. It can be a huge barrier to lifelong learning.

To be a lifelong learner, you need to change your mindset and concepts about it. You need to make learning a priority. There are no rules, no boundaries. You need to embrace this journey and learn about anything from anyone or anywhere. And it is not only about pouring yourself into books but also about things you learn every day from those around you. It is not confined to the walls of a lecture hall.

Great thinkers, leaders and influencers have many things in common. Lifelong learning is one of them. To achieve personal success and to be more valuable and useful to those around you, be a lifelong learner. Do not confine your learning to years or places. Do not confine yourself to learning just from books. All experiences you come across can teach you important things as long as you are open to learning. Always have a strong desire, a hunger for knowledge. Figure out your core reasons why you must commit yourself to becoming a lifelong learner, then write them down in your journal. Without a compelling reason, any habit will not stick. It could be for a better quality of life, for your loved ones, to become financially free, or even to become a better version of yourself. Figure out your 'Why', and the 'How' will become easy.

There is no such thing as failure

In life, you are bound to go through some ups and downs. A strong individual is someone who manages to pull through anything and everything. In order to win in life, you must understand that there is no such thing as failure. The idea of failure is different for everyone. For some people, the idea is quite daunting, while for others, it is just downright depressing and discouraging. Failure comes in different forms. But ultimately, it simply means that you lack certain skills to succeed at that moment. But luckily, you have the power to learn new skills and strive for mastery.

Rejection can be a huge blow if you are not prepared for it. You must always be prepared for rejection because it will come your way at some point in life. Do not be afraid of it, and do not refuse to accept that it has come your way. If you have been rejected from a college, ask yourself why it went wrong. Instead of being afraid of the idea, embrace it and use it as a lesson to make new adjustments.

Everyone develops a fear of failure as they grow older. As a child, you learned how to walk through failure. You tried to get up, but you fell. But did you stop trying altogether? No. You went through a whole process of trial and error to learn how to walk perfectly. The same principle applies to your adult life.

Sometimes, rejection hurts your self-esteem. But if you think of it as feedback rather than failure, wouldn't things be much better? Treat your rejection as feedback and find ways to enhance yourself. Most importantly, do not let the fear of rejection stop you from trying at all. At least give something one or two attempts, if not more. With the right amount of dedication, you will be able to achieve whatever you want.

Failures are stepping stones to success

It is quite a paradox that you must fail in order to succeed. If you fail at something, that doesn't make you a failure. It is a signal that simply tells you that your current approach does not produce the result that you want. By understanding this concept, instead of throwing in the towel, all you need to do is to make new adjustments and try again until you succeed.

A world-renowned example is Thomas Edison performing about 10,000 experiments to come up with the perfect model for a light bulb. What kept him going on after his first or hundredth try failed? The determination to succeed. He did not treat the futile experiments as failures. Instead, he treated them as 10,000 new things that he had learned. There are many examples from history which show that failure is essential in the journey to success. You cannot expect to learn something if your path is obstacle-free.

But when you fail, you see your mistakes, and that gives you a chance to improve yourself. This is why all successful people are so refined in their ways and choices. They have learned from failures in life. Michael Jordan, the famous basketball star, admits that he's only successful because he failed over and over again. You might think failure would only break your hopes and dim the light along the way. Yet, this is not entirely true. It just depends on your own beliefs and perspective.

Learn from the experience

Failure is an amazing experience in its own way. When you fail, you learn new things about yourself. You learn a new way to cope with something and you discover your capabilities that never surfaced before. Just like that, you also learn new things about the task at hand. Learn to strive for progress and not for perfection. Understand that nothing can be perfect, and there will always be room for progress.

One key belief you should implement is this: "As long as I learn from my failures, then I have succeeded." With this little hack, you can never fail! You only fail if you give up. As long as you keep trying, you are not failing.

If your own failures seem overwhelming, then learn from the experience of successful people. They have a habit of never giving up. Instead of being put off by their failures, they use them to their advantage and pave their way to success. They have all taught us that it is okay to fall and that there is no shame in that.

Always remember, your failure is not a stop sign. It might be a sign for you to change your direction or be more focused on the one you are already heading to. But in no way is it a stop sign. If you stop, that is when you fail. As long as you keep going on and becoming better, you are succeeding. Never let others force you into believing that you are a failure. It is your journey, and you know how far you have come. You just need to learn from every experience, and it will soon lead you to success. Everyone faces setbacks in life. But it is people who experiment and persist that become successful later in life. It is only you who determines that you have failed. Not your circumstances or the people around you.

Not everyone gets to play easy in life. Hurdles are bound to come your way. But remember what Tony Robbins says, "There's no such thing as failure. There are only results". In the end, the formula for achieving success is not all that complicated. It is within your grasp once you have decided to go after it with everything you have got.

By following these principles that help you solve problems, overcome frustrations, develop patience, boost self-esteem, and improve yourself as a person, you can be sure that you will be successful in improving the overall quality of your life.

| 7 |

Motivation

Want to be richer? Want to be in better shape? Want to build an amazing business? How about improving your relationships? How about living in an incredible house? All of these goals are achievable. None of them is beyond your reach. And do you know what? You probably already know how to achieve most of them. You probably already have the skills, the knowledge, and the expertise. Of course, you could read a book on each of these topics. You could read a book on how to get into great shape, and you could read another on how to build a business. Chances are you would just be procrastinating. Chances are you will just be spinning the wheels rather than getting down to the actual hard work you know you are really supposed to be doing. You don't have a problem with how. You don't have a problem with what. The issue is with actually doing the things you are meant to be doing. The problem for most of us is that we just lack the motivation that we need to start on a new project. Even if we start out well, we often end up flagging and giving up soon after.

So how do you get around this problem? How do you maintain motivation and drive? How do you stay disciplined and focused?

Grit

With true grit, determination, and willpower, you can accomplish literally anything that you put your mind to. Once you can commit yourself 100% to a given task, who knows what you can accomplish? Grit and determination are not normally spoken in the same breath as "fun" or "relaxation!" However, once you get your motivation and your discipline sorted, you will find that you have more time to enjoy yourself or to relax with your family. That is because you will be able to work more quickly and efficiently, and you will be able to work towards the goals that actually interest you.

I have a real issue with people who say that in order to be successful, you need to sacrifice time with family and friends. It bothers me when people say they cannot be in a relationship because they need to "focus on their career." The reason this bothers me is that I 100% believe (and know) that you can have it both ways. You can work extremely hard on a project you are passionate about and be extremely successful in doing so. At the same time though, you can still find time to spend with friends and family. You just have to work HARD and work SMART and then STOP.

And with this kind of motivation and mental toughness will come all kinds of additional benefits. Firstly, you will find that you become more resilient to things that happen in your life. When you get bad news, you will be able to take it in your stride, adapt, and carry on. When you have more determination, you will be able to improve all your skills through intense learning, analysis, and repetition. When you have motivation, you will be cognitively faster because you will be able to focus on the task at hand without distraction. And you will be able to get out of bed on time in the morning. Clear the kitchen at the start of each day. And bite your tongue in an argument because you are not a slave to your emotions (resulting in many hurt feelings prevented). This will be your superpower. It will change everything for you.

Emotions

Something that shop owners and sellers know about human psychology is that our decisions are driven by emotion and not logic. That is to say, you will buy something not because it is great value, because you need it, or even because you particularly like it. You buy something because you get excited by the cool packaging. Because you think the materials used look elegant. Because you imagine how cool or elegant you will look. You buy it because it is something other people have. You buy it because you have had a hard day and you need a treat. And you buy it because you are worried that it will be out of stock if you hesitate.

Take a look at any marketing materials, and you will see that this is true. The fact is that we are ruled by our emotions, which you can think of as being a compass for the thing our body thinks we should be doing. The problem? Our body is hard-wired to survive in the wild outdoors. As far as evolution is concerned, our main challenges are finding food and staying warm and dry. We want to belong to a strong social group, and we want to be respected by others.

These core emotions can be roughly arranged according to Maslow's hierarchy of needs, but the point is that our thoughts stem from our emotions. And those emotions typically stem from our physiology and environment. For proof of this, consider what happens when you get "hangry." When you become hungry, this will make you grumpy, irritable, and stressed: and this can often lead to arguments, mistakes, and other problems. So, what is actually going on here? First, the lack of food in your system causes your body to release large amounts of cortisol while serotonin levels drop. That heightened cortisol leaves you jittery and anxious, and it is that hormone that causes your thoughts to become stressed and irritable.

Why? Because in the wild, that hunger would be extremely dangerous, and it would be highly important that you seek out food – even if it meant competing with other people to get it. You will now find yourself worrying about your boss firing you, you will think about all the things your partner has done recently to irritate you, and the mess on the side in the kitchen is going to annoy you.

Your thoughts will now begin to race, and you will find yourself struggling to concentrate on anything. You are looking for danger, you are looking for problems, and you are tired. You think you are angry because your boss/partner/housemate is an idiot. But you are actually angry because you are hungry.

So, what does this have to do with motivation and discipline? Why does it matter? The problem is that if you now try to get work done, if you now try to focus, then you are going to find it extremely difficult to do so. Consciously, you want to work on your project and get work done. But subconsciously, you are just looking for food!

There are countless other examples of this. What if you are tired? What if you are cold? Or what if you are stressed about something you said to a friend last week? In these scenarios, the hormones and neurotransmitters running through your body are going to make it very difficult for you to focus on what you need to focus on. Motivation, then, is the ability to overcome that emotional drive to focus on what you need to.

Maslow's Hierarchy of Needs

What happens when you are not hungry? When you are not scared or stressed? When the temperature and your energy levels are just right? That is the point at which you begin to focus on the things that you need to do to be successful: that is the point where your motivation actually comes through.

Remember that hierarchy of needs? It looks like this:

1. Self-Actualization
2. Esteem
3. Love and Belonging
4. Safety Needs
5. Physiological Needs

This list shows us the order in which our "needs" must be met, where the bottom item (physiological needs) takes absolute priority over all else. Self-actualisation is at the pinnacle. This is the feeling of fulfilment that comes from having a goal or a passion. It is self-improvement. It is "the desire to be the most that one can be."

But you cannot be the most that you can be if you are starving to death or nobody loves you. That is why this hierarchy must be structured from bottom to top. You need to satisfy your most basic desires and needs before you can start looking after the soul. The emotional drive to eat will always be stronger than the emotional drive to diet. The emotional drive to be warm and safe will always be stronger than the emotional drive to work out. And the emotional drive to hang out with friends will always be stronger than the emotional drive to go to work.

But it just so happens that the items at the top of the pyramid are also the ones that bring the most lasting contentment and happiness. And this is why so many of us struggle with our motivation – we struggle to tell our bodies that today, comfort and hunger take a back seat to the things we really need to get done to be happy. To improve your chances of going after those long-term goals, you need to hijack your body's own motivation system. You need to force it to sometimes turn the hierarchy of needs on its head.

How do you do that? One option is to try and minimize those nagging doubts and physiological needs.

Physiological needs

In other words, you make sure that you start your day with high-quality food and that you start your day with a clean slate. If you are eating low-quality processed cereal for breakfast, then your body is going to want more sustainable energy and nutrition. Therefore, you will be anxious, and you will struggle to focus on other tasks (even if you are not aware that hunger is the problem). Eat a meal of complex carbs, protein, and fruits, and your body will be satiated and sustained. The result is that you will have one less thing on the back of your mind.

Stress

Likewise, you should try to remove all nagging sources of stress. Tim Ferriss refers to these kinds of issues as "open loops." These are jobs that you know need doing and that are causing mild, low-level stress. Whatever the job, many of us will put off completing these kinds of tasks. In doing so, though, we actually prevent ourselves from focusing 100% on our current task.

Solve this problem by following the "one-minute rule." That means that if a job takes less than one minute to complete, you should do it right away! Now, if you start your day with no distractions and minimal stress, you will be able to focus on your goals much more easily. You will find you are less likely to procrastinate, and you are more likely to get the work that you really need and want to get done.

Environment

Equally important is to consider your environment. Where are you working, and what effect is this going to have on your mindset and your motivation? One big problem that often affects our environment is untidiness. This has the effect of making us feel slightly unsettled and uneasy. That is partly because there is too much visual information to process, partly because untidiness is just tidying work that we know we are going to have to do later, and partly because we might unconsciously associate it with hygiene issues.

And consider this: our peripheral vision is actually more acutely sensitive to movement because we use it in order to scan for danger and predators. You might be focused on your computer screen, but your subconscious mind is scanning the nearby environment for threats and things that need fixing. Fix that now, and you will be much more focused on what you need to get done.

Only once you convince your brain that everything immediately pressing has been taken care of, will it then allow you to focus on the meaningful work toward your goals.

There is another way that you can commandeer your motivation system in order to get what you want. The other thing to recognise is that you will always be more driven by needs that are immediate versus those that pay off in the long term. Sure, if you wake up every day at 4 am and work out, you will eventually be in incredible shape. Probably. But if you stay in bed, you will feel amazing now. Definitely. What wins as far as your primitive lizard brain is concerned?

Think about what already motivates you every day, and then structure that to encourage yourself to work effectively. From a positive psychology perspective, we take Maslow's Hierarchy of Needs a step further. The drawback with it is that it is finite, whereas if you want to motivate yourself and succeed, the self-actualisation stage is an ongoing process. That does not make Maslow wrong, it just means that, if we want to achieve optimum well-being, we need to bear in mind that it is a journey, not a destination.

Visualisation

What happens in your brain when you are motivated toward your major goals and when you are not? How is it that some people are able to push through the distractions of hunger, anxiety, and discomfort and work toward their goals anyway? The reason that our motivation is flexible is that our brain and body don't know the difference between what is happening in the real world and what is happening inside our mind's eye. In other words, we can use visualisation in order to tell our body that there is a threat or a great reward to work toward, and if we are good enough at this, it can become so real that it triggers a huge flood of hormones.

We can use this to our advantage to improve motivation and success. Keep a vision board of things that you are aiming for where you can see them, and every day spend time visualising that you have already received or achieved the items on your board.

Neuroscientists are increasingly subscribing to a theory called "embodied cognition." This states that we think by using visualisation in order to understand the world. What is meant by this? Once upon a time, scientists believed in something called "mentalese." This was the hypothetical universal "machine code" of the human brain. Scientists wanted to understand how humans were able to garner meaning from the conversation and spoken/written language.

In other words, when we understand language, how is this happening? What are we "translating" that language into in order to comprehend it? In lieu of any real answer, mentalese was suggested as a possibility. Embodied cognition suggests that there is no universal machine code and that, instead, we comprehend meaning and language by relating it to our own physical experiences.

We essentially play a little animation of what we are reading or listening to, using our own senses and our own bodies to understand it. So, when someone tells you that they walked through the woods, you understand this by visualising trees and by remembering the feeling of leaves crunching underfoot. When you discuss maths, you understand it by relating that to your own experiences with quantities and objects.

Our understanding is routed in our physical experience (even if we are not consciously aware of this happening). Brain scans appear to confirm this theory or at least lend support to it. They show that when we hear a story or think about something, areas of our motor cortex and sensory cortices light up as though we were using them. And as such, as far as the body is concerned, there is little difference between thinking about walking through a cold wood and actually walking through the wood. The experience is very similar, and as such, the hormonal response is also very similar!

This is how you can motivate yourself to do something. When you think about what could be gained by working on your physique or by working on your business, you will visualise that endpoint (again, this might happen unconsciously). This can release a huge amount of dopamine (the reward hormone), which controls motivation and goal-oriented behaviour.

This will then activate a pattern of activity in the brain called the "salience network." This is the part of the brain that causes us to switch attention from one thing to another and then to hold that focus. This network is made up of the executive control network (conscious control of attention and motivation) and the dorsal attention network (reflexive response to stimuli). One of the key brain areas involved in this is called the anterior cingulate cortex.

When that part of the brain is damaged, it can leave a person with absolutely zero attention or motivation – they find it impossible to stick to tasks and eventually become completely inert! So, how, then can you use visualisation in order to work toward your goals?

The first tip is to make sure that the thing you are working toward is something that you feel extremely passionate about. This is perhaps the most important way to stay motivated and disciplined: to have an end goal that you truly care about. One that you get excited thinking about. You need a goal like that in order to stay motivated. What if you don't know your "life purpose" or end goal yet? Even working toward a short-term, immediate goal will have similar benefits. Just make sure that there is always something you are working on and toward. You need to make sure that this goal you are working toward is something that speaks to you emotionally. That means it should be something you feel will help you become actualised.

In other words, the more of your needs the ambition and the goal meet, the greater your chances of success. What if the thing you are working on doesn't have any emotional payoff for you? What if you need to focus on a project given to you by your manager? Notice how this is the kind of work you really struggle with? The answer is:

1. Think about the reason you need to do this work. In this case, focus on what career success might mean for you.
2. Try to do the work you are doing more inherently engaging. If you are writing a dull article about something you don't care about, try to find what is exciting about that topic. Or challenge yourself to write the very best article with the best structure and the best grammar possible. This will help your work to truly come alive.

Fear

Humans are naturally risk averse. Again, this is an evolutionary hangover that once made a lot of sense in terms of our survival. We couldn't afford to take big risks with our safety or our resources, and so we would cling to things we needed. This was effective back then, but today it has the effect of making us somewhat static and unchanging. We are happy to stick with the status quo because at least it is safe and predictable.

A small amount of stress – called eustress – is a positive thing. (Too much is bad for motivation, but this is something we will address in an upcoming chapter.) Another thing to consider is the threat of not progressing. What happens if you don't work on your fitness? Simple: you stay out of shape forever and get progressively worse. You never fix your self-esteem, and you create more and more health problems that make it even harder to turn things around. What happens if you never start applying for other jobs or negotiate higher pay? You potentially remain stuck in a dead-end job for the rest of your life! Or at least miss out on huge amounts of money that could make you and your family much happier. Those are some very compelling sticks! In the latter example, the hope is that the threat of being stuck in the same position forever is enough of an emotional motivation – a tangible enough vision – to override the slightly awkward thought of having to talk about salary with your boss/clients.

Priming

Another tip is to use something called "priming." Priming means getting yourself into the right mental state for the work you need to complete. (Not to be confused with neural priming, which is a completely different – though interesting – topic.) For example, if you need to work out but cannot muster the motivation to do so, you can always try watching a motivational video of someone training instead. Likewise, if you are struggling to stay focused on your work, you could watch a video of someone else being productive.

Doing this helps to light up the right brain areas; our mirror neurons and natural empathy help us to feel as though we are working on the thing we need to work on. Similarly, you can also motivate yourself by using the right environment. We already discussed how you could remove distractions and thus make it easier to concentrate on what you are supposed to be focused on. But how about tuning the environment to support and encourage maximum productivity?

This concept was explored in-depth in the book "Deep Work" by Cal Newport. There, the author discussed the possibility of creating a space designed entirely around the concept of encouraging productivity and inspiration. This space included areas filled with inspirational items and great works, for example, that would help to inspire and subtly influence the person trying to be productive.

We can create something similar in our own office environments and even our own gyms – by filling them with things that will make us feel productive and inspired to do our best work. So, by considering all these factors, we can "hack" our motivation and become the most productive and hard-working versions of ourselves. Not by reasoning with ourselves and trying to convince ourselves to work harder but by making the work we are doing become the thing we cannot stop thinking about.

Energy

Let's say you have a goal that you are entirely focused on and extremely passionate about. You have cleared your schedule, and your home is perfectly conducive to that writing/productivity/training. But you still cannot find the motivation to get productive. Why not?

How about this: can you give me 100 push-ups right now? Unless you are in the car or on the train, there is not much of a good reason why not. But I bet you don't do it. (Go on, I dare you!) So, what is stopping you now?

The problem very often comes down to energy. And this is another aspect of motivation that is so often misunderstood and overlooked. Too many people claim that they don't manage to achieve their goals because they don't have enough time.

"I don't have time to work out."
"I'd love to learn a language, but I don't have time."
"There is not enough time in the day to look for a new job."

None of this is true. You can always find more time in the day. You can look for a new job while you are commuting! You could get up 15 minutes earlier to do a workout. You could learn a language on Bluetooth headphones while you cook. And I bet that you have spent plenty of time doing other things. Watched any good TV shows recently? Have you not wasted any time on Facebook lately? So, if there is time, then why is it you cannot do the thing that you want to do?

The answer is energy. Energy is finite. You cannot simply keep piling more and more on top of an already packed schedule and expect not to be tired. The reason that you come home from work and then just want to crash on the sofa is that you are too tired to do anything useful. Even to do something useful like reading!

The more tired you get, the more your motivation and willpower are depleted. This is why we are more likely to snack in the evening. We even start making more selfish decisions come evening, according to studies! Even if this is something you really want to do, when you are tired, your body is going to want "brainless" activity. So, what do we do? Sometimes, no matter how much you try to cajole or trick your brain into wanting to do the thing you are telling it to do, you just cannot manage it. This is certainly true when you are trying to fit more into your routine than you realistically can.

What is the secret? One such answer is to make the things you want to achieve work around your existing routines and energy levels. Very often, your energy problem is actually a stress problem. That is because stress is something that can affect us all differently but which is always emotionally exhausting. In a moment, you are going to learn how you can motivate yourself in order to gain more energy and strength. But the same is also true: bad news, an argument, or a stressful thought can all take the wind immediately out of your sails. So, learn to protect against these things using meditation and mindfulness.

The other option is to find ways to wake yourself back up. One of the best options? A little bit of physical exercise. Often, we don't want to exercise because we are too tired, but as soon as we start, we feel more awake again. Exercise increases the demand for blood around the body and muscles, which in turn accelerates the heart rate and breathing. This sends signals through the vagal nerve to the pituitary gland, triggering a release of adrenaline and related hormones. This makes you stronger, more energetic, and more awake.

Start with light exercises – such as some stretching or a little bit of light bouncing up and down. Don't even demand anything more of yourself than that! This can then give you enough energy to do more should you wish to. It can also help you to gain more energy for a host of other tasks. This is one reason that office workers are often encouraged to get up and walk around the room at occasional intervals.

Not in the mood to jump up and down even? Cannot think of anything worse? Then you could always try a trick from the animal kingdom. It is called "pandiculation," and it essentially involves stretching or not stretching exactly. Not reaching your toes and then holding that position for 2 minutes. Rather, it means stretching, as in a yawn. As in the way that your cat or your dog will stretch when they first wake up after a nap. This movement involves elongating the body with a slight muscle contraction – and it feels extremely invigorating. The reason for this is that you are contracting and then relaxing the muscles in order to help let go of stored tension. This can help to immediately remove stiffness – stiffness that otherwise can easily be mistaken for tiredness. Not only that, but it also helps to "wake up" the connection between the brain and the sensory-motor cortex. When we don't use the muscles for a while, this can lead to something called sensory motor amnesia. By contracting the muscle, the connection between the brain and the limb is reinforced. In fact, a yawn is actually a form of pandiculation, which helps to release tension in the respiratory muscles: including the intercostal muscles (which expand and contract the chest to open and close the lungs), the jaw muscles, and the diaphragm. If you are planning on doing something physical but you cannot muster the energy to do it, then try stretching.

Finally, another way to wake yourself up when all you want to do is to curl up in a ball is to splash some cold water on your face. The reason for this is that we have lots of very sensitive nerve endings in the face, which, when stimulated with cold water, can trigger something called the "mammalian dive reflex." This effectively increases blood flow to the brain and can trigger a flow state – not to mention waking you up and helping you overcome any lingering sense of fatigue.

Physical effects of motivation

Did you know that motivation can make you physically stronger? This is where stories of mothers lifting cars off of their children come in. And it is not impossible: a shot of adrenaline helps to increase muscle contraction and maximise strength. Did you know that it is possible to reduce the physical symptoms of alcohol intoxication simply by willing yourself to? Have you ever noticed how you can quickly sober up when something bad happens on a night out? All this shows the power of motivation and will. It shows that if you are excited enough, then you can trigger enough of an emotional response to overcome even physical ailments.

So how do you get to this point? Options include using motivational videos again, using music, or just having a pep talk with yourself. Remind yourself why you are doing this, what the consequences are if it goes wrong, and what the emotional hook is.

It can be hard work motivating yourself to work when you really don't want to. But while that may be true, it is also fair to say it is much harder to trek through the desert for days on end without sleep. To run over barracks into enemy fire or to make life-or-death decisions when your body is screaming at you to sleep. Of course, I'm talking about the military. I'm talking about paratroopers. I'm even talking about Spartans.

For centuries, countries have been training their military to not only be able to fight but also to be able to do so in the direst and most stressful circumstances.

What is the secret? Partly, the secret comes down to learning to be comfortable in the uncomfortable. This has even been occasionally referred to as "discomfort training." The truth of the matter is that we always want to be comfortable. We want to return to the homeostasis that we now know signals that all physiological needs are being met.

While this is true though, it is also true that the human body was not designed to always be comfortable. Think about your ancestors. They did not have central heating, they did not have warm baths, and they did not always have clean clothes. The strange thing? They were no less happy than you! This is habituation. We become used to what we have, and that then becomes our "baseline." Our bodies have adapted to living in warm, soft environments where everything is set at the same height as us. We have very little physical or physiological stress. This is all well and good, except it makes us highly susceptible to any fluctuation in what has become our norm. Now when the heating breaks, or when you find yourself a little bit over-tired, you feel as though your world is coming apart. Your body triggers a major stress response, and you feel anxious, jittery, confused, angry, and sluggish. So many of us struggle to perform on less than adequate sleep!

Meditation

You need to do something to cultivate the right mentality to begin with. One way to do this is through meditation. Because meditation is a practice that involves focusing the mind, this can be achieved by focusing on a mantra (such as "om"), listening to your own body, or chanting a prayer.

These are all different types of meditation, but the goal is ultimately always going to be the same: to change what you focus on and thereby change your mindset. What you will find is that meditation can help you get through the toughest grinds in your life. Why? Because you can simply choose to detach yourself from the fear, from the boredom, or from the pain. When you do this, you can rise above stress and even find a way to thrive amidst the chaos.

Mindfulness – a meditative practice that involves focussing on the here and now – has a lot in common with stoicism. Stoicism is a philosophy that suggests we cannot avoid hardship, nor should we want to. All we can do, therefore, is to change the way that we respond to it. This is our obligation, and by doing so, we can work through the very toughest of times. Developing a stoic mindset can be accomplished through practising meditation and learning to direct your thoughts toward more positive things.

Motivation and goal setting

When it comes to staying motivated, there is a right way and a wrong way to set goals. The right way is to set a goal that you feel comfortable you are able to complete, that you have total control over, and that you can quickly assess. The wrong way is to set a distant goal that you think you might one day be able to accomplish, that is vague and idealised. So, a good goal is something like: I will exercise three times a week for the next month. I will only have one snack a day. A bad goal is something like: I will lose three stone by next year.

The problem with the latter goal is that it is so distant and reliant on so many factors that it comes down to much more than just motivation. Often, you might find yourself excusing yourself from training or from eating correctly because you believe that the goal is so far away you can excuse yourself. Also, when you check in and find you haven't lost any weight at all after the first month, you might just give up! And what if you have a bad week where you were unwell? Or perhaps if you went on holiday? This setback could again completely destroy any motivation and sense of progress you had built up.

Conversely, a good goal that challenges you to do something (or not do something) every single day, will be extremely easy to measure. Not only that, but each day presents a fresh challenge. Fell off the wagon today? Then you can just try harder and do better tomorrow. And there are no excuses. You cannot "exercise three times a week" later. You either succeed or fail, entirely based on your own commitment.

Each day is a fresh challenge for your willpower, and all you need to do is to focus on that "here and now goal." Of course, you will still need that endpoint in mind. You still need the emotional hook and the goal to work toward. But you are not going to concentrate on that. You are only going to concentrate on the daily grind. When you check in a year later, you will find that the "end goal" has taken care of itself.

While the bulk of this chapter has been about understanding how your motivation works, how to tap into it, and even how to grind through the truly unpleasant work, it is also important to recognise that there is a flip side to motivation: the rest and the relaxation. You might not think that this has any business in motivation, but the truth is that you cannot have one without the other.

When you force yourself to be disciplined, it is useful to think of this as using up sand in an hourglass. You only have so much sand that you can work through before the whole thing needs to be flipped and reset. How do you reset the hourglass? Simple: by relaxing, by spending time with friends, by sleeping, and by recovering.

Focussing on these eventualities – knowing that you will eventually be able to rest and will get to enjoy yourself - is a fantastic way to give yourself more motivation through the hard times. What is more encouraging? "I need to keep going forever, no matter how tough it is!" or "If I keep going for another hour today, I can relax and enjoy my favourite book tonight." In fact, did you know that the key to muscle growth is actually to rest and recover better? Muscle doesn't grow during workouts; it grows after them as long as you provide enough protein. The same is true for grit and determination. Learn to balance the yin and the yang and to keep the two separate!

Motivation and determination are things that can be learned rather than being hereditary or genetic. The key is to understand what makes your own mind tick and to learn the crucial role of emotion. When you do this, then you can tap into those emotions and trigger them as needed. Practice meditation, and learn to be comfortable with being uncomfortable. If you can do these things, then you will gain a kind of grit and determination that makes you capable of truly anything.

| 8 |

Positive Emotions

Positive emotions are emotions we find pleasurable. Feelings of happiness, excitement, joy, hope and inspiration are all positive emotions. Positive emotions are key to a happy and healthy life and to achieving optimum well-being. They help us perform better in all areas of life and make us optimistic and filled with hope.

How and how often we experience positive emotions is different for everyone, but if we are able to maximise our positive emotions, we are much better placed to deal with negative emotions as they happen. The gradual accumulation of positive emotions over time will lead to increased well-being and greater happiness.

Another benefit of increased positive emotions is that it improves performance by as much as 20-30%. Research by Professor Barbara Frederickson, through her Broaden and Build Theory, has found that heartfelt positive emotions alter the way your brain performs by flooding the brain with dopamine and serotonin, the feel-good chemicals, and this may help you process new information.

Earlier, we looked at motivation. Positivity increases motivation through your mindset and the way your brain responds to opportunities and challenges. It changes the boundaries of your mind for impacting your future success and well-being. According to Professor Frederickson, positive emotions:

- Broaden your mind
- Build your resources
- Short-circuit stress

Another aspect of positive emotions is the way they are found to be contagious. We tend to mimic the moods and facial expressions of those around us, whether positive or negative, so by smiling, we make others smile too.

To find out your positive and negative emotions ratio, try the brief Positivity Ratio Test at https://www.positivityratio.com/single.php It takes about 2 minutes to complete and will give you a good indicator of how positive you are. Studies have found that individuals who achieve a 3:1 positivity ratio tend to be more generous, caring and dedicated in their actions, which in turn makes them feel good and achieve greater success.

Happiness

Positive emotions direct our feelings toward happiness. We go through life doing our best to reach our dreams and our goals. We think that once we have achieved success, we will finally be happy and at peace with the world. This may be true. However, the simple fact is that not everyone is going to end up successful.

Only a small minority will reach the pinnacle of wealth and power. Most of us are going to get stuck living mediocre lives. So, the question is, does that mean only a small percentage of people are going to live happy lives? Are the rich, powerful and successful the only ones with the right to be happy? The answer is, fortunately, no.

You need neither money nor power to have a happy and fulfilling life. After all, happiness is a state of mind. You can have all the money in the world and still be unhappy. On the other side of the coin, you can have no worldly possessions but still live a very happy life. Your happiness is not dependent on money, career, or status in life. It starts with you.

We all have different definitions of happiness. What might make you happy may not be a source of happiness for other people. What others call their source of joy and fulfilment may be a source of disdain for you. For instance, many may say their happiness comes from their families and their good health. For others, it might be their jobs and their careers. For some, it is their wealth and their social standing in the community. For more than a few people, tasty food and drinks light them up like no other. And the list goes on.

With that said, researchers have long debated a single definition of happiness. This is because there are far too many factors that affect and contribute to a person's happiness. The consensus, however, is that "happiness is the state of being happy." I know this definition still seems a bit vague, but the point is that happiness is a mental state that reflects the range of emotions you encounter on a daily basis. It defines how you view your life, that is, whether you are satisfied or unsatisfied with your quality of life. If you are dissatisfied, then obviously, it means you are not happy.

Now the thing is, just because someone is happy doesn't mean they are going to be immune to negative emotions. Nothing can be further from the truth. Happy people still encounter trials and challenges, but they deal with these differently than unhappy people would. This is what sets them apart from the rest of the population. Happy people are not deterred easily. They are less susceptible to negative emotions. They don't allow others to walk all over them. Their happiness is contagious, and people naturally gravitate towards them. You know a genuinely happy person when you meet them. They can literally light up a room just by being in it.

No matter what your personal definition of happiness is, this simple truth remains: we can all use some more happiness in our lives. The world will be a much better place to live in if everyone on this planet radiates happiness. When you are constantly feeling the blues, and you cannot remember the last time you felt happy and free, then you need to figure out why as soon as possible. Getting stuck in an unhappy state is not ideal for anyone, as unhappiness can quickly spiral into depression. Here are a few questions you can ask yourself to figure out what is causing your unhappiness.

Are you doing what you want to be doing?

Ask yourself this very important question. If you answer "no," then what are you doing about it? Are you taking any steps towards the job or career you want? Or do you feel like you are trapped in a day job you don't particularly like, but you stay in it because it pays the bills? For many people, this is a common dilemma. They know they are not happy with their current jobs, but they stay in it year in and year out. They may not like it, but they feel like they have no other choice. Over a period of time, their day jobs become their comfort zone. They become afraid of pursuing their passions. If you are one of them, then you need to figure out how you can free yourself to pursue your interests and your passions in life.

Can you not find a way to pursue your passion? What steps are you taking to free yourself? Your answers will hopefully help you see the light, so you can finally start pursuing the career that will make you happy.

Are your thoughts making you unhappy?

You have a say in what goes on in your mind. That is, you have a choice about the kind of thoughts you allow to run through your head. You can choose to think positively, or you can choose the opposite. If you choose the latter, then it is going to make you unhappy. You can tell yourself to stop thinking negative thoughts. But this is easier said than done. We can tell ourselves all we want, and the negative thoughts will continue in the background.

Visualisation plays a vital role in overcoming negative thoughts. But it is also important to be self-aware and to pay attention to your thoughts. There is a trick you can try right now: Every time you catch yourself thinking negatively, tell yourself to stop. Take a deep breath and imagine your whole body coated in Teflon and the negativity sliding off you and banished from your mind. You can then let your positive thoughts take over.

Aiming for perfection

There are lots of things you should be aiming for – perfection is not one of them. Why? Because when you set perfection as your ultimate goal, you are inevitably setting yourself up for failure.
Instead of perfection, aim for something more realistic, like excellence, for instance. It is still higher up on the achievement scale, but at least it is more attainable. Not a single one of us is perfect, so why aim for perfection?

When you aim for excellence, however, you give yourself a fighting chance to succeed. You are not going to be scared to go out there and mess up because you know your chances of making it are good. You use your mistakes as learning experiences. And the other benefit of aiming for excellence? You have always got some more room to grow! You can be the best performer at work, in school, or in your sport and still have the opportunity to do an even better job next time.

Once you have figured out why you are unhappy, you will be able to move forward and finally be on the path to creating happiness in your life.

Be grateful

When your unhappiness is eating away at your soul, and you think everything you have is going to waste, think again. Look around you. What do you see? What do you smell? What do you hear? When was the last time you looked at the sky? Really looked at it. Can you appreciate the sound of leaves rustling in the wind? Or the feel of grass on your bare feet?

Now, imagine having all these taken away from you. Imagine losing your vision, your hearing, your sense of touch, your sense of taste, and your sense of smell. Take a moment to reflect on what you are missing out on. Imagine spending the rest of your life without all of your senses. It is extremely hard, is it not? Fortunately, the above is just an exercise. But a powerful one at that. I hope it made you see just how trivial your problems probably are compared to having everything – literally everything – taken away from you.

Your comfort zone

Staying in your comfort zone is just as important as leaving it from time to time. Contrary to popular belief, your comfort zone is not fixed to a single location. It is not bounded by physical walls. The truth is that our comfort zone exists in our minds. With that said, it should be easy to get out of it, right? Unfortunately, the answer is "no." It is far more complicated than that.

Comfort zones are called 'comfort' for a reason. It is where we usually head to the moment life becomes too much for us to bear. It is your 'usual' environment where you control everything. But this can become a negative place when it holds you back from living life the way it is meant to be lived. It is true that you can be happy inside your comfort zone. But, like most things in life, you need to work on maintaining that level of happiness. And in order to do that, you need to step out of your comfort zone.

Do not let your comfort zone drag you down. You know what you want deep down inside, but you are too afraid of all the risks and the unknowns along the way. A realistic method of going after your dreams, and minimising the risks, is by planning. Have a solid plan on how you are going to get from point A (where you are now) to point B (your big dream), and break it down into milestones and mini-goals. Every time you achieve a milestone, it brings you one step closer to your goals. Just take it easy. Have a daily, weekly or monthly goal, and you won't even realise how far you have left your comfort zone behind!

When making your plan, ask yourself what your greatest fears are and why you fear them and then figure out how you can combat these fears. If you are afraid of public speaking, perhaps it is because you hate the thought of people laughing at you. To face your fear, try thinking of it this way: you have a very important message to share, and the only way people are going to learn about it is if you go out there and tell them. Otherwise, they are going to live their lives in blissful ignorance. Also, you can say to yourself that maybe half of your audience is in the same boat as you. They are just as afraid of public speaking as you are. Whatever your fear is, break it down until you can see how insignificant it all is in the grand scheme of things!

Learning new skills

Learning a new skill in this day and age is a must. Employers value it, colleagues appreciate it, and best of all, you are not limiting yourself to a single skill. New skills will open up a whole new world for you. If you want to succeed in life, you need to pick up as many relevant skills as possible. In short, you can never have too many skills.

Change

There are two kinds of change: positive and negative. It may not always be evident at first; that is, you are not sure if the change you are embracing will lead to good results or bad results. Sometimes, you need to take a leap of faith and just do it. When dealing with change, you can initiate it, or you can wait for it to happen. The good thing is if you initiate it, you are in a much better position to control it rather than just reacting to it. It is also easier for you to adapt to the change because you are expecting it. Though change is often painted negatively by naysayers, there are actually plenty of benefits to embracing change. Here are some of them:

New opportunities

There are opportunities everywhere. When you allow yourself to embrace change, it is easier for you to uncover hidden opportunities.

Some people may even say the opportunity will reveal itself to you. This is because when you embrace change, you open your eyes as well. Where everybody else is running away from the change, you are walking towards it with eyes wide open. This makes it easier for you to spot new opportunities.

Personal growth

Failure to embrace change means you are going to get stuck doing the same things over and over again. There is literally no room for you to grow and improve as a person. Often, the only way to progress is by welcoming change.

Discovering your strengths and weaknesses

Accepting and embracing change will allow you to discover your strengths and even your weaknesses.

Problem-solving

When you don't resist change, you will eventually figure out new ways to solve problems. Getting exposed to new environments helps you think outside the box. Change can bring out your creativity. It enables you to seek new solutions more efficiently and effectively. But, if you refuse to accept change in the first place, you will be stuck troubleshooting the same old problems.

Creating a life of happiness means embracing change. It means stepping out of your comfort zone. Ask yourself, what can you change in your life right now that will lead to your ultimate happiness?
Do you need to change jobs? Do you need to take up a new hobby? Do you think moving to another city or even another country is necessary

for you to achieve happiness? Only you know the answer to this question.

The important thing to remember is that seeking and embracing change should be on top of your list if you really want to achieve true happiness.

Negative habits

If you want to create a life of happiness, then it is imperative that you start working on getting rid of your negative habits and replacing them with positive ones. However, doing this is clearly not as simple as it sounds. It is because negative habits take time to build. It doesn't happen overnight. Instead, it occurs over a period of time. You don't need to think about it; you just do it. That's when you know you have formed a habit.

Negative habits have the undesirable effect of making you unhappy in the long run. Breaking negative habits will take time. You need to work on it, and you need self-control and self-discipline to be able to put a stop to it. Here are a few strategies you can use to help you say goodbye to your negative habits:

- **Know your cues**
  Experts say habits have three parts: a trigger or cue, a routine, and finally, a reward. Knowing what your cues or triggers are is the first step to overcoming a negative habit.
- **Stress**
  Sometimes negative habits form in response to various stressors in our lives. If you find yourself responding negatively to stress, then it is time to do something about it. How? By trying your best to reduce your stress levels.

Figure out what makes you stressed and try to find a way to avoid these situations to make your stress levels go down. In most cases, living a stress-free life is not going to be possible, so you need to face it head-on and learn to control or manage your stress. We will explore this further in another chapter.

- **Anchor your habits**

  One of the easiest ways to break a negative habit and replace it with a positive one is to use an 'anchor' system. This is how it works:
    - every time you catch yourself starting to do the negative habit, you do the new one instead. For instance, you are trying to break the habit of, say, biting your nails. Let's say this negative habit is triggered by stress. Now, you also want to build a more positive habit of reading or listening to inspirational content to help you grow as a person. Every time you catch yourself biting your nails, you stop, and then pick up a good book nearby and read a few pages. Or you can go on YouTube and listen to your favourite motivational speakers. After a few weeks of doing this routine, you will be able to remove nail-biting from your list of negative habits and end up more inspired and less stressed in the process.

- **Make a list**

  There is a reason why negative habits are called 'negative'. They have undesired effects that may or may not manifest immediately. Write all the negative consequences down and use them as your "why" for why you should stop the habit. Make your descriptions as detailed and as graphic as possible. Every time you make a mistake and you go back to your old ways, look up this list and make a promise to do better next time.

  Re-examine your life from time and time and assess if you have any habits left that need to be stopped. Of course, it is entirely possible you will pick up some other negative habits in the future, even if you end up turning your life around and living a happy existence. That is okay. No one is perfect. Just pick up where you left off and never stop working on making yourself a better person every day.

Learn to love yourself

Loving yourself is a prerequisite to creating a life of happiness. This is because you can only be truly happy and at peace with the world if you love yourself first. Likewise, you cannot fully love another person if you don't even appreciate yourself to begin with.

With that said, how do you know if you love yourself enough? Here are a few tips:

- **Love what you see in the mirror**
  You don't need to have the most beautiful or the most handsome face in the universe to appreciate your looks. You also don't need to have a supermodel's body to say you look sexy. We cannot all be fortunate enough to win the genetic lottery. But, the truth is, even those we think look 'perfect' have insecurities as well.
  We think that making ourselves look perfect is the only way to appreciate what we see in the mirror. But when we are constantly comparing ourselves to somebody else, and we are always spotting imperfections even when there are none, then we will never be satisfied with our looks and ourselves. You will always find something to criticise.
  Cosmetic surgery may have come a long way, and you can now transform your physical appearance to your ideal one, but at what cost? The good news is you absolutely don't have to. You just need to work on accepting yourself for who you are, that includes your looks. Whether you like it or not, it is the face you

were born with. Learn to look beyond the physical. Sooner or later, you will be comfortable in your own skin, and the mirror will finally become your friend.

- **Put yourself first**

    Prioritising yourself over others is not a sign of selfishness; it just means you love yourself more than others. However, if you take it to an extreme, that is, if you step over others to get what you want, then it is a different story. But if you are not hurting anyone, then it is okay.

    The problem with most people is that they are too afraid to hurt others' feelings. They follow their parents' wishes and their spouse's demands. They easily bow down to peer pressure even though they know what they are being asked to do goes against their values.

    Giving in to people you like and love is okay, but don't make it a habit. Your so-called friends can easily exploit your trust. If you don't learn to stand up for yourself and fight for what you believe in, they can easily manipulate you to do their bidding. Letting others walk all over you is not a sign of selflessness. You are a breathing human being. You have your dreams, your goals, and your own life to live. Don't waste your time making others happy if you yourself are not happy to begin with. If you want to devote your life to making others happy, you need to be in a position of loving yourself fully first.

- **Taking care of your health**

    Nothing says self-loathing louder than letting your health go to waste. The old cliché is true: your body is your temple. If you don't take care of your body, then it means you are not taking care of your temple. You don't need to sign up for a gym membership right now. Neither do you need to buy all organic food from this point onward. Taking care of your health simply means paying attention to your body and its needs. Make a habit of eating healthy food and stop eating junk food. Stop doing anything that degenerates your body.

Learn to listen to your body. When you are stressed and tired, take a nap. Take a day off. Go away for the weekend. Sometimes, you may also want to do nothing at all for the whole day. Give yourself some room to breathe. You not only get to have fun, but you also give your body a much-needed break from the hustle and bustle of your daily routine.

Positive relationships

Material possessions can indeed make you happy, but not nearly as much if you share those possessions with people you love and respect. After all, we are hardwired to thrive in human contact and relationships.

We will explore positive relationships in much more detail in a later chapter.

Making the right choices

We make decisions throughout the day. Most don't require much thinking; you know exactly what you are going to do. But in many cases, you need to stop and take some time to mull over your decision, where you weigh the pros and cons of all the options available to you.

When the stakes are higher, and you stand to lose something valuable, making the right choice is of utmost importance. Losing is never fun, especially when it means sacrificing something important to you. For example, if you make the wrong decision, your job, your relationships, your happiness or even your life could be at stake.

In some decisions, you know what the outcome is going to be right away; it is clear-cut. However, for some decisions, the outcome won't be known until a certain period has passed. So, how do you know you are making the right choice in life? Here are two signs you are making the correct call:

1. *Instinct*

   You have probably made decisions before where deep inside, you absolutely know you are doing the right thing (even though your mind says you are making a mistake). And it turned out that you were right! In most cases, you probably didn't even know why you made that choice, you just know that deep in your heart it was the right call. Some superstitious people may say it was your guardian angel or some higher, invisible power telling you what to do. But those who believe in science say it is a combination of past experiences and knowledge. Our brains somehow connect the dots and interpret the data to tell us what to do. There are countless stories of people who have listened to their intuition and lived to tell about it. They have somehow managed to avoid accidents, disasters, bankruptcies, and other equally life-changing (or life-ending) events. So, if you are faced with a difficult decision right now, try listening to what your gut says.

2. *Feeling proud*

   If your decision is something you can live with, then it is a good sign you have made the right choice. But if you are going to be ashamed of it, then obviously it is the wrong one.

Analysis

Big decisions need analysis. Write down the pros and cons of each option. Then sit on it for a few days and come back to it when you have thought things through. In the end, what is important is that you go after what is going to make you happy. You may ask other people for their input, but remember, it is your life, and your actions will impact you more than anybody else.

Kindness

Paying it forward simply means doing the same favour you have received from someone else to other people. For instance, someone did a small, kind favour for you today. Instead of paying back that person, you do the same kind favour to someone else. Paying it forward is a very powerful concept. One random act of kindness has the power to change someone's day for the better.

Imagine if everyone in the whole world practised this concept. One good deed can touch billions of people! While we can only dream about living in a much better world, paying it forward can truly make a lot of people's lives better. Your generosity and your kindness are going to make others happy. But will it make you happy as well? Research says yes. Giving makes you feel good about yourself. It makes you feel fantastic that you did so something that helped somebody and made them happy in the process! Being kind has a lot of tangible benefits. Here are some of the top ones:

- ***It makes you happy***
  Some people say kindness is overrated because it sets you up as an easy target for abuse. This may be true, but then again, there is no rule book that says you have to be kind to everyone. Not everyone deserves your kindness. The moment you feel like you are being taken advantage of, just move on from that person. There are plenty more people who will appreciate your help and will be more than willing to pay your kindness forward. These are the people you should strive to help out. With that said, when you help people who truly need your help, you will feel a deep sense of happiness and accomplishment that you are not going to find anywhere else.

- *Relationships*

    We naturally gravitate to people who exude positivity, and that includes the people we view to be good and kind. While it is true you should only help someone because you want to help, not because you are expecting anything in return, the fact remains that being kind has a few side benefits. These include making others feel 'close' to you. They feel like you are a kindred spirit, someone who understands their struggles and is willing to help them out in times of need.

    No matter how angry or upset you may be at someone, if they do a good deed that benefits you, it ultimately makes it easier for you to 'forgive' them. In short, kindness can mend and improve relationships. Try doing a random act of kindness every day for a few weeks and see if that doesn't turn into a good habit. When you have made kindness a habit, your self-satisfaction is going to be at an all-time high. The people whose lives you have touched in one small way or another are going to be grateful to you. You will make new friends.

    You will be happier. You will be a more positive person. You will be a joy to be around with. Don't expect anything in return, though. If the people you have helped continue to pay it forward, you are making your community – and the world - a much better place. No matter how small or insignificant you think, your act of kindness is, continue doing it. You may not know it, but all these small things are going to add up, and your kindness will come back to you when you least expect it. It is how karma and the universe work.

Gratitude

We have come across the concept of gratitude in previous chapters, but it is particularly relevant when we examine our positive emotions. Gratitude is the unique quality of being entirely thankful for what you have, as well as always being ready to appreciate and help others. Gratitude is one of the primary keys to living a happy and prosperous life of optimum well-being. When you show gratitude for what you have, you are content with your life and positive about all that it has to offer.

If you feel a lack of gratitude in your life and are afraid that it may be creating a void, it is time for you to take action and learn how you can develop gratitude to live a happier life. If you are currently in a difficult situation in your life and think that it is impossible for you to be thankful, then now is the time to cultivate gratitude and achieve greatness. With determination and effort, you can quickly develop a sense of gratitude and become content with yourself and your life.

If you are ready to improve your overall well-being and live a happier life, then you can learn to cultivate gratitude and achieve greatness. Gratitude, like any skill, can be learned and you can develop habits of gratitude. With practice, gratitude can become a choice. You can learn how to bring gratitude into your life and improve your relationships.

Almost every day, we say thanks. We absentmindedly tell it to the grocery store checkout operator and to the barista at our local coffee shop, but are these sincere expressions of gratitude, or merely a response we have been conditioned to give?

What exactly is gratitude? Is it something different than saying "thanks," or is the "thanks" a component of gratitude? As you will discover as you read through this chapter, a simple "thanks" can have a powerful impact on both the person communicating their appreciation and the person receiving that appreciation. This is especially true when a genuine emotion of gratitude backs the word. The question then becomes, what exactly is gratitude?

The Roman philosopher, Cicero, described gratitude as the greatest of virtues and the parent of all others. It is the key that opens all doors and is the quality that makes us and keeps us young. This statement, spoken more than two thousand years ago, is quite compelling. It speaks of gratitude as a virtue or quality of being. Gratitude is just this and so much more. Gratitude is also an emotion. It is something that we feel deep in our hearts. We can feel it toward others, when people are grateful to us, or when we see a person express gratitude toward another.

As a sentiment or as an exchange between people, there is a simplicity to being grateful. And yet, when trying to understand this simplicity, we can find a more complex meaning. Gratitude is an emotion, it is an experience, and it is a conscious choice for awareness. Connections in your relationships are both strengthened and fostered with gratitude. At its core, gratitude holds an experience of universal belonging.

We can experience a real sense of overall well-being when practising the intentional cultivation of gratitude in our lives. Take a moment and shut your eyes and try to recall a time when you felt appreciated. Remember this event as if it were happening at this very moment:

- What words did you hear?
- What did your body feel like at that moment?
- What triggered the experience?
- What were you thinking at that moment?
- What did you enjoy most about being appreciated?
- What about this particular moment brought you to remember it today?

Write down your answers to these questions in a notebook that you can refer back to later.

There is not a single definition of gratitude. Gratitude has been conceptualised and defined in the context of attitudes, emotions, morals, traits, habits, and even coping techniques. Gratitude is without a doubt, an incredibly complex and dynamic emotion. It is a skill that contributes to satisfaction in relationships and human excellence.

Gratitude as an emotion

In this context, we need to be sure to distinguish emotion from mood. Emotion is about something or someone. It is about a personally significant circumstance or experience. A mood, on the other hand, is not connected to any object and is not dependent on any one thing.

By exploring gratitude in this way, we can see that it occurs in response to an action within the framework of a relationship. Something has been given by someone and received by someone else. This exchange helps to foster the emotion of gratitude.

Gratitude is an empathic emotion, which means that in order to experience the emotion in exchange, the receiver needs to place himself in the position of the giver. A feeling of gratitude in response to a gift requires the recipient of the gift to sense the giver's positive intention. It is this recognition and empathic connection that provides the foundation for the emotional experience of gratitude in the interaction.

We can express gratitude for any number of reasons. We can be grateful for receiving personal benefits, such as advice from a mentor, or we can be grateful for material items, like a gift, our home, or a car. Gratitude can also be fostered through interpersonal fulfilment, such as getting a hug from a friend. Or, we can experience gratitude for a monetary gain. In today's highly consumerist society, where quarterly growth figures have become a measure of a nation's standing or where possessing a killer instinct is considered a great asset, the question then becomes whether gratitude has a place in our society.

While we are all still pursuing happiness, our ways of finding it varies. For some, we try to obtain it through service and charity, while others try to find it in esoteric books and from gurus. Unfortunately, for most of us, we try to find happiness through material acquisition. This has turned our society into one that feels it is entitled to all it receives and obtains and shuns the idea of expressing gratitude for all that we have. Things are now viewed, by many, through the prism of sales and purchase, and some even view both relationships and possessions from a use-and-discard perspective. Thankfully, gratitude is just as contagious as materialism. As soon as you realise that, gratitude can help you reach the happiness and greatness you have been chasing.

Gratitude and relationships

It is easy to get caught up in the hectic routine of everyday living and forget to express our appreciation to those that matter to us the most. Take a moment to think about the relationships in your life and consider a time when you felt gratitude for those people.

One of the most common mistakes we can make in our relationships is the assumption error. This occurs when we assume that someone in our life knows what we are thinking or feeling, or when we believe that someone else should know what we are thinking or feeling. The problem with this is that if we don't let those people in our lives that are important to us know that they matter, they don't know that they matter.

For most of us, we have stopped being consciously aware of our lives. Our brains and body have become so familiar with our routines that we put little thought or attention into our daily lives. Our minds are usually busy making lists, recalling events of the day, or thinking ahead that we have stopped being consciously aware. We tend to go through the emotions that we know so well and miss out on all the nuances of the experience in the process.

Having an increasing awareness of gratitude can have a ripple effect throughout your relationships. There is evidence that when we share our gratitude, whether in kindness, words, or gifts, we nurture our relationships, helping them to grow stronger and closer. Knowing this, it makes perfect sense that we need to explore how we can convey our appreciation to those that matter the most to us. While there is nothing wrong with expressing your gratitude by saying, "thanks a lot" or "nice work," these expressions of gratitude are often taken for granted and seldom convey the message as powerfully as we want.

One way you can verbally express your appreciation in a manner that will foster connection in your relationships is by including three things in your expression:

1. Observation
2. Feeling
3. Need.

In sharing your observation, you state what you observe, like holding the door open or emptying the dishwasher. These everyday actions do make a difference, but they often go unacknowledged. Sometimes just letting someone know that you noticed can make a world of difference to that person. Next, you need to let that person know that what they did has a positive impact on you. The final aspect of communicating gratitude is often the trickiest. It can be difficult to acknowledge that we need others, but we do.

It is important to remember that we don't exist in little bubbles and that we are consistently affected by those around us. Letting someone know that they were there when you needed them is a good way to establish a connection with others.

When it comes to thinking about your own relationships and opportunities for gratitude, don't limit your expressions of gratitude to the things that people give you or do for you. Sometimes it is just as valuable to share your appreciation for who they are as a person. Let the people in your life know that you appreciate not only what they do for you by who they are as well. Take the time to comment on someone's generosity, thoughtfulness, compassion, or just being who they are, and see how much happier you become in your relationships.

Positive emotions and gratitude

Wanting to be happy is not an unrealistic desire. However, we are often misinformed about what happiness is. At times, we may think that we can find happiness in a new computer, a new shirt, or a new car. Other times, we may believe that indulging our impulses will make us happy. While these things in and of themselves aren't bad, you need to consider if any of these things have brought you truly, lasting happiness. A study of twins has demonstrated that approximately 50% of happiness levels are based on genetics. This means that there is some predisposition to happiness, but that also means that half of our happiness is not wired into our DNA. Another study determined that our life circumstances, like wealth, relationship status, health, etc determine 10% of our happiness. This means that if 50% of our happiness can be attributed to genetic makeup and 10% to circumstances, that leaves a massive 40% of our happiness up to us and our behaviour.

This 40% means that we have a significant say in how happy we are in our lives. We have a choice. What does this have to do with gratitude? Well, it turns out that research has shown that grateful people are indeed happier people. Gratitude can reduce the frequency and duration of depressive episodes, which makes a lot of sense because it is hard to feel bitterness, anger, envy, hostility, and resentment when you are feeling grateful. By its nature, gratitude has the capability to block more negative and unpleasant emotions. When it comes to gratitude, it is essential for you to realise that the feelings you experience are valuable and that they all serve a purpose.

When you feel afraid, you may become anxious. This emotion puts your body in a state of alertness, so you are ready for anything and can grow in tune with your surroundings. Feeling anxious when you are walking down a poorly lit street at night is an appropriate emotion and can help keep you safe. That same feeling of anxiety prior to speaking publicly can prompt you to prepare for the event and help you to have an excellent presentation ready to go.

Emotions that are typically referred to as negative are merely more unpleasant to experience. Bitterness, sadness, guilt, regret, shame, envy, resentment, and anxiety are not necessarily bad, but they can be uncomfortable to experience. Your mind is, to some extent, programmed to focus on these emotions and give them more of your attention. This is because these are essential emotions in that they give you valuable information about yourself and how you are responding to your environment. Without these emotions, you wouldn't know if there was danger lurking around the corner or if you are viewing something that is opposed to your moral and ethical views. These emotions can prompt you to take action.

Gratitude and other positive emotions don't discount the negative experience but can help you keep things in perspective and keep you from getting stuck in those negative emotions. Practising gratitude is one way to transform your experiences toward more positive emotions and improve your relationships. If you work with appreciation, you will begin to shift your experience toward the positive.

Benefits of gratitude

Gratitude has also been proven to increase our capacity for experiencing other positive emotions. Often, gratitude is described with the same feelings connected to it, like love, compassion, humility, comfort, passion, and confidence.

Cultivating gratitude can be a direct way to enhance these other emotions in your life. Another benefit of gratitude that several studies have supported is that grateful people are more resilient and resistant to stress. When you can find the ability to be thankful for the things you have in your life, you find yourself able to move through challenges and difficulties in your life, time and time again. Gratitude helps us see our strengths, open our hearts, and experience the fullness in our lives. Gratitude is an opportunity that is there waiting for you every day.

Gratitude can be learned. With practice, gratitude can be a choice, an intentional way of viewing the world. This is not to say that you should discount or make light of difficulties or painful experiences in your life, but you should choose not to let yourself become overwhelmed in these times and find a way to see beyond them. You can look with gratitude at what you learn about others and yourself when you are moving through hardships.

Meditation and mindfulness

It is amazing how often we adopt someone else's emotional story as our own. When we hear it and witness it often enough, we will begin to fall into those same patterns. Whether it is a habit and pattern of complaining or of doing things a specific way, to some degree, we all pick up on the habits and behaviours of those closest to us.

While this is not necessarily a bad thing, it is something that we can benefit from being more aware of. If we don't know that we are doing something or why we are doing it, it can be difficult to tell if it is effective for us or how it may affect our relationships and experiences.

How can we recognise these patterns and "borrowed" patterns? How do we move from the less effective patterns and move to cultivate an attitude of gratitude? There are many ways that you can progress toward this, but to build awareness, the best path is through mindfulness practice.

We have already discussed what mindfulness is in a previous chapter. Taking the time to focus your attention intentionally can change the imbalance of the chemical circuitry in your brain and help you to shift out of your negative thought patterns. Other research has discovered that mindful awareness practices can enhance the body's general functioning and, promote healing, immune response, stress reactivity, and provide you with a general sense of physical well-being. You will also be able to improve your relationship with others when you practice mindfulness because it allows you to be better able to recognise nonverbal signals from others but also acknowledges your part in the interaction.

Because our lives can get quite hectic, we tend to go on autopilot and miss opportunities for connection and gratitude. Sometimes, we even miss what we are experiencing at the moment. Taking a few minutes every day to stop, slow down, settle our bodies, and actually pay attention to the moments can have a profound impact on how we feel about the day and what we did to fill it. Our thoughts, emotions, and behaviours are all connected. Each one feeds into the others and shapes our experiences with others and the world we live in.

Practising mindfulness helps us notice our experiences, our relationships, and our environment in a different context. With mindfulness practice, we can pay attention to our thoughts, behaviours, and emotions without judgment. When we are mindful, we begin to see our world and notice all the opportunities for gratitude that exist. Any daily routine, task, or errand can become an opportunity to practice mindfulness and gratitude. You can practice mindful gratitude anywhere at any time. If you are struggling to incorporate mindfulness into your daily life, you can use meditation to train your brain to do it automatically.

Mindfulness can be cultivated through mindfulness meditation, which is a systematic method for focusing your attention. You can learn to meditate on your own, following instructions in books or through the help of videos and tapes. Some types of meditation involve primarily concentration, like repeating a phrase or focusing on the sensation of breathing. This concentration allows the constant flow of thoughts that inevitably arise to come and go. Concentration meditation techniques, as well as other activities, can induce a relaxation response, which can help to reduce your body's response to stress.

Mindfulness meditation builds upon concentration practices. Once you establish concentration, you begin to observe the flow of your inner thoughts and emotions without judging them as either good or bad. Then you start to open your mind and notice the external sensations around you, such as sights, sounds, and touch, that make up your moment-to-moment experience.

The challenge in mindfulness meditation is to not latch onto any one particular idea, sensation, or emotion or get caught up in thinking about the past or future. Instead, you should be watching what comes and goes in your mind to discover which mental habits produce a feeling of well-being or one of suffering. There are going to be times when you don't feel as though this process is at all relaxing. However, over time it will provide you a greater key to happiness and self-awareness as you become more and more comfortable with a broader range of experiences.

Gratitude meditation is one of the most influential and rewarding exercises you can do. When you are able to develop an attitude of gratitude, you can start feeling more content with your life and accomplish true happiness. Gratitude can make you feel good, and meditation will help you to achieve a deep state of relaxation and contemplation.

Gratitude and meditation can be incorporated together, or you can spend a few minutes at the beginning of your meditation session taking deep breaths while you think of all the things that you are grateful for in your life. You can start your gratitude meditation practice by taking a few moments to do some deep breathing relaxation techniques. Start by breathing in through your nose. This will extend your abdomen and cause your diaphragm to pull air into the bottom of your lungs, which will provide your body with a healthy dose of oxygen and help you to become more relaxed.

When you are ready, sit in a comfortable chair, one that is suitable for meditation, and close your eyes. Allow your muscles to begin to relax. Let go of your thoughts. When you feel relaxed and comfortable, start to think about everything that you are grateful for in your life. The more that you are grateful for, the more you will receive in your life. Whether you choose to practice gratitude meditation or gratitude relaxation and breathing on a regular basis, the happier and healthier you will be.

Unbalanced gratitude

So far, you have discovered that gratitude has a number of positive attributes and benefits. You have learned that people who are grateful tend to be happier, healthier, and more satisfied in and with their relationships. Gratitude opens us up to being able to connect with others and can help us through stressful situations and experiences. However, it is entirely possible to experience, or at least express, something similar to gratitude without the benefits.

For gratitude to occur in your relationships, there has to be an exchange from one to another. There must be a giver and a receiver, and there has to be an awareness of that exchange. When the awareness of the gift is not present, the exchange becomes unbalanced. This can result in either a missed opportunity for gratitude or even a false expression of gratitude. Unbalanced gratitude, or unhealthy appreciation, occurs when there is a sense that one should be grateful, but the feeling is not there. It is the thought of, "I know I should be grateful, but I cannot help but feel (guilty, awkward, suspicious, resentful)" or some other variation of a feeling of unease.

Superficial gratitude is one that is not genuine or from the heart. It occurs most frequently when there is a public expectation or demand for acknowledgement. The best example of this is the yearly award shows that are aired on television. The words of gratitude are present, but the sentiment behind those words is often non-existent.

The challenge with this kind of gratitude is that it seldom makes you feel good. It doesn't come with the added benefits of the other emotions that are so often associated with gratitude; emotions of joy, happiness, love, connection, and even hope. Instead, superficial expressions of gratitude are often associated with a feeling of anxiety and resentment. You can also end up with superficial gratitude when there are too many people to thank, more for the reason of not wanting to exclude anyone. When there is a long list of thanks being recited without the connection to what is being acknowledged, the sense of appreciation becomes diluted and has less meaning. There are many situations where you may feel pressured to offer thanks, even when you are not feeling the emotion, which can lead you to another form of false gratitude.

Obligatory gratitude shares some similarities with superficial gratitude. There ends up being an overwhelming sense of "should" behind the expression of thanks rather than a genuine feeling of appreciation. This kind of gratitude often occurs when you feel a need to say "thanks" for a kindness that was received but one that was not wanted or needed. You may feel obligatory gratitude when you feel obligated to thank someone for a gift that you neither wanted nor liked, or when someone is doing something for you that you want to do on your own.

Rebuilding the balance

Everyone, at one time or another, has experienced unbalanced gratitude. The critical thing to understand is that it is not true gratitude. Whether the false gratitude is stemming from cultural expectations or an intention to be perceived as better than another, it is missing the essential elements of the components that are necessary for gratitude to be sincere. If you find yourself engaged in an exchange of unbalanced gratitude, it is up to you to look for ways to restore the balance.

Empowerment

On a psychological level, practising gratitude allows us to become happier, more positive, and more amenable to finding joy and pleasure in everything that we do. Showing gratitude for the things we have and those around us also has social advantages as well because we become more generous and compassionate in our interactions with the world around us. Studies have shown that gratitude helps us on both psychological and physical levels. Physically, when we practice gratitude in our lives, it can help to boost our immunity levels, which in turn can lead to us living a more healthy and more energetic life.

Gratitude can empower you to understand better that life is all about the moments lived rather than continually looking out for the good or bad moments. Gratitude teaches us to be grateful for all the moments that make up our lives. Gratitude can help you develop an optimistic and positive perspective on life, even with all of its ups and downs. Living life with gratitude will enable you to understand and appreciate that taking the rough with unruffled patience is the key to your happiness, contentment, and peace. Instilling an attitude of gratitude in children from an early age will help them value the blessings they have, leading them away from the sense of entitlement that affects so many today. It has become far too easy for children today to take what they have for granted.

This ingratitude ends up putting them on a path that is difficult for them to find peace and contentment, which could impact their ability to have meaningful relationships in their lives, both at work and at home. The best thing about the empowering nature of gratitude is that it makes you view your own self in a new light. The more thankful you are for everything that is good in your life, the less you will dwell on those aspects of your personal life that falls short. Gratitude will also make you a more empathetic person who can appreciate the achievements of others without feeling envious. This can free you up to focus on doing the things in your life that work for you.

Among the many beautiful ways that gratitude can empower your life is the way that it ends up energizing your being. The very act of embracing the positive and letting go of the negative can make you view your life with hope and optimism, which provides you with enthusiasm to give your best in everything that you do.

Meaning

Life is more than the relentless pursuit of material possessions and achieving goals. Having a sense of gratitude for what we have and wishing the best for everyone else puts us on the path of self-realisation, allowing us to have contentment as a constant part of our life, as well as enabling us to reach out to those who may need your help. People who practice gratitude have more positive energy and tend to be more popular because of their more pleasant and affable personalities. This can help you make more friends and have a deeper, more meaningful connection within your relationships. In general, grateful people are more helpful, more social, more trusting, and more appreciative.

Learning gratitude

Thankfully, gratitude can be learned. With the right application of practice and discipline, you can master an attitude of gratitude in your life. The thing about gratitude is that it may not be all that challenging for most people to express when things are going well. However, the moment a crisis occurs or an unhappy situation arises, people don't see much reason to be grateful. Many would rather complain about their life. The thing about gratitude, however, is that it is nothing more than a state of mind. You can, if you want, find a reason to feel grateful even in the darkest of hours. No matter how terrible things may seem to be, there is always something for you to be grateful for. The thing to remember is that we are all on this planet for a short period, and as long as we live and breathe, we have something to celebrate. If things have gone wrong, you have to remember that they can also get better.

When you take some time to observe the way grateful people conduct themselves, you will start to notice similarities in their behaviour. Life rarely happens in the way you expect. The best students in school don't necessarily do better in life. There are numerous instances where somebody less talented than you is able to land the job that you wanted or who find more success than you. No one knows what sort of cards we will be dealt with in life. When you are prepared for the surprises that life will inevitably throw at you, you will always be able to find a silver lining and be grateful.

When you put a prior condition on being happy, you will likely never reach that happiness. There is nothing wrong with coveting a particular sports car, but if you decide that you are going to be depressed until you get it, what would happen if it suddenly goes out of production? People who readily show gratitude for whatever good they see in their lives, no matter how small it is, are those who find it rather easy to be happy. Unconditional gratitude is definitely one of the prerequisites for living a happy life. People that can appreciate that the good comes with the bad will find that their hearts are grateful for the good in life while realising and understanding the fact that there will likely be a corresponding downside. People who find it easy to express gratitude for the smallest bit of happiness don't get fazed by the changes in life. They are eternal optimists who only need the slightest glimmer of hope to be happy and content.

Gratitude is something that we have endless opportunities to feel each day. The challenge becomes not getting caught in the negativity bias of our brain. The negativity bias is our tendency to focus our attention on the more uncomfortable emotions such as fear, anxiety, anger, and sorrow. While these emotions are essential for us to because they prompt us to pay attention to things that may be threatening or dangerous, we shouldn't live in them or let them be the ones that inform our entire life experiences.

With practice, you can develop new patterns of thinking and new ways to experience your life. Just like with a new diet or exercise, engaging in a new behaviour for one hour, one day, or one week, will not create a long-term change, but regular practice can create a sustainable change. It can quickly become a habit. Something that you do automatically. No matter what your situation, there is always an opportunity for gratitude. Even the most frustrating experiences can offer you a chance to practice gratitude, but they can also allow you to observe it and be influenced by its presence.

Any new behaviour or routine will take time to develop into a new habit. Developing a habit of gratitude will require some attention and effort on your part. While shifting gratitude into a consistent practice does take effort, it is a worthwhile investment of your energy. Research has shown that in addition to increasing your awareness of the abundance already present in your life, practising gratitude gives you a wide range of benefits, including:

- Improved ability to manage daily stress
- Increased optimism about the future
- A heightened sense of community
- Increased resiliency to traumatic events
- A heightened sense of emotional well-being
- Increased physical activity
- Improved sleep
- Improved physical health
- Reduction in feelings of depression
- Reduction in feelings of anxiety
- Positive impact on both cardiovascular and immune functions

It is critical to remember that habits take time to develop. There may be days when you forget about gratitude altogether. That is alright. You can pick up the practice again the following day. Over time, the practice of gratitude will become more automatic. Just like learning anything new, you have to give yourself patience and time to develop gratitude habits. With continued practice, you will notice the rewards in your own life unfold.

Giving

Entitled is a word that is used to describe many children and adolescents today. Entitlement is one of the most significant obstacles to gratitude. When you believe that everything is owed to you, how can you feel grateful or genuinely appreciative? This belief of deserving blocks gratitude. So, the question becomes how you can shift from an attitude of entitlement to one of gratitude. There are several ways that you can accomplish this. First, you can start by adjusting your own attitude and modelling a grateful attitude in your home. You can also teach your children about gratitude and giving rather than about deserving and owing. The key to teaching gratitude is to engage in activities and interactions that are focused on sharing, giving, and connecting rather than doing something in order to get something back.

As much as we live in a world where we are conditioned to give thanks, often without awareness, we also live in an age of entitlement, where more and more people are finding themselves disappointed because they are not receiving what they believe they deserve. Believing that the world owes you anything is a false premise and will only lead you to experience disappointment, strains in your relationships, and further resentment and frustration.

Writing it down

As you look for ways to combat entitlement and foster gratitude in your life, you can look to the simple act of writing thank-you notes.

Often, when people talk about writing thank-you notes, they are taken back to when they were required to write obligatory thank-you notes for graduations, birthdays, and weddings. In these situations, writing thank-you notes can feel a bit daunting and can quickly become overwhelming. In many of these situations, the gifts that are purchased are out of a social obligation, and the thank-you notes are also written from a place of social responsibility. While this may not be representative of sincere gratitude, it is a positive step in moving toward developing gratitude habits because it is a way to acknowledge gifts received.

But you can go a step further and move past obligatory gratitude and into reflective gratitude. Reflective gratitude happens when you are able to step back from a situation, recall the event, and re-experience the emotions that occurred during that moment or span of time. Often, we don't realise the benefit that we are receiving from someone until after we have had time to reflect. Thank-you notes have a positive effect on those who receive them.

Taking the time to reflect on the relationships you have developed and the gifts that those relationships offer you can move you from a place of resentment or victimisation into feeling appreciative of the gifts that you have received. It can also provide you with the opportunity to reflect on how you have affected those around you.

Putting it into practice

Now is your chance to practice cultivating gratitude in your life. his can be done by yourself or with others. The trick is to practice. As with any new skill that you are learning, developing an attitude of gratitude is going to take time. By incorporating the following practices into your everyday life, you will find that, over time, you will experience the world a little bit differently. You will begin to see opportunities hiding in the most obvious places. You will notice richness in your relationships, and you will start to feel more connected to those around you.

Not all of these practices will be comfortable for you, and some might even make you feel a bit silly doing them. That's alright. Keep trying them. Some of these exercises will resonate with you, while others may not. The key to cultivating gratitude and achieving greatness is to keep practising until it becomes intuitive. As discussed earlier, meditation and mindfulness are essential aspects of finding gratitude in your daily life. If you are not familiar with the practice of meditation, these exercises may be a bit challenging. If your thoughts begin to wander, or your mind goes into judgment and questioning mode, that's alright; merely redirect your attention to the practice at hand. It is essential that you be gentle with yourself. There is no right or wrong way to do these exercises.

Gratitude journal

For this exercise, you will need to purchase a notebook or journal to keep by your bedside. Each evening, prior to going to sleep, sit quietly and bring your attention to your breath, keeping your head relaxed.

Think through the events of your day. Visualise those events as they occurred, be sure to pay close attention to moments that contained acts of kindness, laughter, or beauty. As you notice these occurrences, pay attention to how your body feels. Pay attention to the sensations that you are feeling. What kind of thoughts arise in your mind?

When you have completed reviewing your day. write down the observations in the journal. Also, start noticing the things that occur each day for which you are grateful. These things can be big or small; it doesn't matter. The magnitude of what you are identifying is not essential, but instead that you are noticing things that you can appreciate about the day. You may be grateful for a person, for opportunities that were presented to you, for a good cup of coffee or tea, or perhaps that the day has come to a close, and you are now preparing to lie in your bed and rest your head on your favourite pillow.

Every night, before you go to sleep, write down the things that you were grateful for throughout your day. Again, these can be big or small; it doesn't matter. Write down at least three things every day and once a week, sit down and review your journal entries.

To get you started, here are 10 things you should appreciate in life:

1. **Life**
   Every day you wake up, you are given another lease of life. You have a new opportunity to start your life anew, to make amends, to make an impact in this world. Instead of trudging through your day as though you are carrying the weight of the world on your shoulders, try to live each day as though it were your last. Every single day you live like this is going to be your best day ever!
2. **Family**
   No matter how busy life gets, always find the time to connect

with your family. Everyone in your family helped shaped you to become the person you are today.

3. **Friends**

Having friends you can count on is important. They can improve your life, and likewise, you can help enrich theirs as well. Have meaningful conversations with your friends.

4. **Health**

Good health often goes unacknowledged. Learn to take good care of your body. We are only reminded to be grateful for our health when we become ill.

5. **Love**

Whether it is romantic or platonic love, self or selfless love, the saying "love makes the world go round" holds plenty of wisdom. Love makes you come alive.

6. **Laughter**

There are lots of things to laugh about in this life. Laughter has plenty of benefits, including making you healthier. When you laugh, you reduce your stress levels. When you share a laugh with another person, you immediately feel a bond with that person.

7. **Tears**

Tears may be seen negatively, but sometimes tears are necessary. It helps put things in perspective. It helps you appreciate life and laughter even more.

8. **Nature**

While there is less of nature now than there was a few centuries ago, there is still plenty left to appreciate. Even if you live in a city, you can still take some time to appreciate the greenness that plants and trees bring. Observe and be amazed at how nature takes back what is hers in abandoned places.

9. **Time**

We don't have an infinite supply of time. The truth is, the moment we are born, our bodies start counting down how much time we have left. We don't know exactly when it is going to end, which is why we cannot let trivial problems in life bring us down. Let's enjoy the limited amount of time we have here on this planet.

10. **Yourself**

    Yes, you. Learn to appreciate yourself. You are not perfect; nobody is. But you have come a long way. Think about all your successes and your failures, your hopes and your dreams. Then think about the people you have met along the way and how you have helped them in one way or another. Think about the legacy you are going to leave behind.

Learn to appreciate everything you have in your life – both good and bad. In the end, they all come together to provide a unique life experience that is meant to challenge you and bring out the best in you. When you stop worrying about everything and start appreciating every little thing in life, your happiness will become apparent, not just to yourself but to everyone around you, too.

Breathing

Even on the busiest of days, there are small moments where you can practice gratitude. Take a moment, two or three times a day, to slow down and bring your full attention to your breathing. Notice each breath. Observe every inhale and exhale, noticing that at that moment, you don't have to do anything but breathe. Once your breath has your full attention, silently say the words "thank you" on each of the next five to eight exhalations as a gentle reminder that right now, at this moment, you are okay. These silent "thank-yous" can serve as a quick reminder of the gift of your breath and how lucky you are to be alive. Do this practice at least three times per week.

Remind yourself

It is extremely easy to forget something, especially when you are trying to form a new habit. Placing visual reminders around your home or workspace can help you stay on track with your goals.

Create reminders that will prompt you throughout the day to think about gratitude or merely to pause and reflect. Here are some ideas for your gratitude reminders.

- Carry a small stone in your pocket. When you notice the rock, pause for a moment and reflect on gratitude.
- Place a note on your office wall, refrigerator at home, or bathroom mirror that says, "I am grateful."
- Set the alarm on your phone to go off one or more times a day as a cue to pause and reflect on gratitude.
- Schedule a five-minute "gratitude break" in your office calendar two or three times each week. Use the calendar reminder feature to help keep you on track.
- Have a "gratitude partner," someone with whom you check in daily to help identify aspects of gratitude in the day.

| 9 |

Health

Have you heard other people talking about optimal living and wondering what it is and whether it could help you to achieve more of your goals in life? In this chapter, we take a closer look at what optimal living is all about and how you can make changes to your life to exploit its full potential.

Optimal living, at its heart, is all about finding the perfect balance in your life to help you achieve the goals that you have set for yourself. It is about becoming more productive and more successful and forging stronger and more positive relationships in every area of your life. Working towards continuous improvement is at the core of optimal living.

Of course, living optimally is not something that always comes to us naturally. We must implement changes to improve our mental and physical well-being, and we can do this by implementing certain lifestyle choices. The modern world is a hectic and frantic place. We are all working harder than ever before, trying to achieve more in our working and personal lives while striving to stay fit and healthy both mentally and physically at the same time.

Simplifying how we live our lives can make a huge difference to the way we face the world, and this is where implementing some healthy lifestyle choices can prove indispensable. These simple methods are quick and easy to implement but can simplify and improve how we live exponentially. You will find that you will soon see positive changes across all aspects of your daily life.

Sleep

Sleep is a vital element for both physical and mental well-being. Without enough sleep, you cannot function effectively daily. Not only does a lack of sleep negatively impact your productivity at work and home, but it can even cause you some serious medical issues. Poor quality sleep can lead to mental health problems such as anxiety and depression, not to mention physical issues such as hypertension and heart disease, which can have severe and lasting repercussions.

However, while we know that we should all be getting 7-9 hours of sleep every night, it can be difficult to achieve that goal. Whether you work shifts, have family responsibilities or are struggling to get all your school or college work done, fitting in enough rest can be a serious challenge. So, how can you resolve that problem? The answer could lie in tracking your sleep patterns.

Thanks to the latest technology, you can have access to sleep-tracking functionality at home. You can now buy wearable sleep trackers that will keep track of your sleep patterns so that you can become more aware of the length of time you sleep, the stages of sleep that you reach and the quality of sleep that you have enjoyed. These days, we can customise more things in our life than ever before. We can personalise our clothes, phones and homes, so it makes sense to be able to personalise your sleep patterns too. Not all of us need the same amount of sleep every night, but if you track your patterns, you can come to a better understanding of how many hours is right for you.

If you are having sleep problems, a wearable sleep tracker will help you to pinpoint the cause of your sleep issues. At one time, the only option was to go to a sleep lab to get a professional assessment. Now, you can have similar functionality in your own bed. With the accuracy and accessibility of modern sleep trackers, you can spot problematic patterns and change your habits for the better. If you track your sleep patterns, you will also begin to wake at the optimal time. Many of the best sleep trackers have a smart alarm to wake you when you are during the lightest sleep stage. This stops you from waking groggy and irritable. Instead, you will feel ready and rested from the get-go for a more productive day. If you invest in a sleep tracker, you can improve your sleep quality and, in turn, the quality of life you can enjoy.

More of us are more stressed and anxious than ever before, so getting enough quality sleep is imperative. If you are sleep-deprived over extended periods, you are vulnerable to medical problems, both physical and mental. Heart disease, respiratory disease and type 2 diabetes have all been linked with insomnia.

While we are very aware of what we are doing during the day, during the night, our routines often get lost. We are used to monitoring behaviour patterns during the day, from what we eat to how much exercise we get, so we should start to do the same during nocturnal hours. If you track your sleep, the greatest benefit is that you will start to spot links between your sleep patterns and overall wellness. For example, you will discover whether drinking coffee or consuming caffeine negatively impacts your sleep or whether the alcohol that you drink affects the quality of your rest. You will also find out whether the time at which you exercise affects your sleep patterns, whether exercising in the evening or morning is most beneficial for you. You will be able to see if there is a link between your use of devices and computers and the quality of your sleep and how much your sleep, or lack of it, correlates with the stress and anxiety levels you experience. You will even be able to determine whether eating late in the evening or whether certain foods affect your sleep, and for women, whether their menstrual cycle causes their sleep quality to fluctuate. By pinpointing these patterns, you can then easily choose to adopt changes in your lifestyle that will not only help you to sleep more effectively but will also help you to be more productive, more fit and healthy and more positive in all areas of your life.

On the other hand, that doesn't mean you should sleep for an incredibly long time. If you sleep longer than your body actually needs, then you can become sluggish and listless, which can also lead to stress when you are unable to meet deadlines, get through your personal to-do list or simply feel down that you aren't being productive. Oversleeping can make you just as irritable and stressed out as not getting enough sleep.

To determine just how much sleep your body needs, it is important to establish a regular sleep schedule, even on your days off. It will force your brain to go into shutdown mode at the same time every night, regardless of what you have planned for the next day. Once you make this change and catch up with your sleep, you will find that you are less stressed and, overall, much happier.

To establish a regular sleeping pattern, you will just need to do a few things every day:

- **Avoid any exercise about 2-3 hours before your scheduled bedtime.** Exercise creates endorphins that give us energy. And while that's a good thing, you want to give your body adequate time every night to wind down.

- **Have a warm bath.** Consider taking one with some essential oils an hour or so before bedtime. Vanilla and lavender are naturally calming scents, plus they complement each other very well.
- **Food.** Try having a banana or two, or a handful of peanuts, about three hours before bedtime. These foods contain tryptophan, which after being consumed, creates melatonin: a hormone that makes us sleepy. But avoid eating too close to your bedtime, as doing so can cause heartburn and acid reflux.

Blue light

More of us are now becoming more aware of how blue light can affect our bodies, yet with increased device usage, we are exposed to more of it than ever before. To enjoy maximum well-being, we need to find ways to minimise the amount of blue light we allow ourselves to be exposed to. Understanding how light interacts with our eyes is the key to knowing why blue light is so bad for our well-being. Light is made up of different coloured waves, which all have different energies. Red light is at the beginning of the visible light spectrum. This has low-energy waves and is easier on the eyes, particularly during the night. Blue light, however, has the highest energy waves, and this makes it more difficult for the eyes to process effectively.

While high-energy light waves are vital for our daily lives, it can prove to be harmful if we are exposed to them at the wrong times. High-energy light is received from the sun to regulate sleep patterns effectively. In the day, the light enters our eyes to release enzymes, bring our levels of melatonin down and help us to wake up.

Melatonin regulates our sleep cycles via circadian rhythms. However, this cycle is all too easy to disrupt. Excessive exposure to blue light can disrupt your circadian rhythm cycle severely. This is because it reduces the melatonin levels released by your body. If your body does not have enough melatonin at bedtime, you cannot sleep properly and become exhausted.

Blue light is emitted by screens from laptops, smartphones and tablets and eventually causes eye strain, near-sightedness and dry, itching eyes. Even worse, blue light affects the cellular anchors and the retina and can cause Advanced Macular Degeneration at a younger age. Some experts have even linked obesity to melatonin disruption as well as the development of some forms of cancer.

Finding ways to avoid excessive blue light exposure is, therefore, essential. Some manufacturers of devices are now recognising the harm that blue light can cause us and are starting to develop new technological solutions to resolve the problem. Blue-filter covers are available for purchase for VR goggles, mobile phones and laptops, and some devices have now integrated "evening modes" into their design which filter out the blue light when you use your device in the evening hours to limit your exposure.

Of course, the obvious solution to the blue light exposure problem is simply to avoid using any device during the evening or night. Smartphones and tablets should be kept out of the bedroom, and for several hours before bed, we should steer clear of any device usage. Unfortunately, this is not always practical or even desirable. So, how can we avoid the issue? The answer could be to invest in a pair of blue-light protective glasses. These are designed with an HEV (high energy visible light) filter built in. These allow you to use your devices whenever you like without any worries about exposure to blue light impacting your sleep patterns. Blue light blocker glasses look the same as a standard pair of glasses, but they have special filters that prevent high-energy visible light from reaching the back of the eye. They can either be purchased as a standalone pair of glasses or as a special pair of night-time glasses which can be worn over a regular pair of spectacles. If you put these on around an hour before you go to bed, they will block all the blue light emitted from your devices and LED lights helping you to get better sleep every night.

Morning routine

When you are starting a day, try never to start it on a bad note. Typically, if your day starts well, then the rest of the day doesn't seem so menacing, and you can better handle situations you face through the morning, afternoon, evening and night. Don't tackle anything stressful in the morning. Things you know will take a long time and hard effort, save for after your morning routine.

Most people assume that time for yourself is at night or in the evening when the day comes to an end. While this is an understandable assumption, time in the evening should be dedicated to wrapping up and completing your day. The best time to spend on yourself is the morning when the sun is high and the day begins. That is why it is better to start your days earlier. Starting them earlier gives you more time to yourself, enough time to make the morning an enjoyable routine rather than one you resent.

Set yourself a morning routine of 20 minutes or so that you make a habit of going through before you do anything else. The exact routine is up to you but could be along the lines of:

- As soon as you wake up, do a morning gratitude meditation. If you finished the previous evening by writing down three things you were grateful for, then you will still have this on your mind when you wake up, so that is a good place to start.
- Say some positive affirmations
- Drink water
- Move your body to music
- Eat a nourishing breakfast

The first thing that you will notice is how your productivity levels rise. Busy lives cater best to those who wake up early. Looking at well-known success stories, most such individuals report waking up at 5 am or even earlier. Apart from the obvious benefit of gaining more clock time hours added into the day, early hours also means fewer distractions. The mind also tends to be more alert in the morning and allowing for focusing better than when surrounded by interruptions. Thinking clearly also goes to benefit better decision-making and increased productivity during the day.

Exercise

We all know that we should get plenty of physical exercise to stay in peak physical and mental shape. However, regardless of this widespread knowledge, many of us still are not getting the recommended amount of activity on a daily or weekly basis. The next important health benefit to add to your life is to add more exercise every day.

You will probably have heard in the media that too many of us are living a sedentary lifestyle but what does this mean? Sedentary lifestyles are defined as a way of living where you don't do enough physical activity regularly. The current recommendations are that we should all do at least 150 minutes of moderate exercise every day or, alternatively, 75 minutes of vigorous exercise. Walking around 10,000 steps every day is recommended as the optimal goal to improve your health and to reduce the possible health risks which occur as a result of inactivity.

The WHO (World Health Organization) says that up to 85% of the world's population is not physically active enough, and this makes the sedentary lifestyle the fourth top risk factor around the globe for mortality. Traditionally, we are led to believe that eating healthily and doing some aerobic exercise can offset all the effects caused by spending excessive time sitting down. However, evidence now shows that if you exercise for half an hour a day, you still may be unable to mitigate the potential damage. The best solution appears to be to reduce the amount of time spent sitting down and increase the amount of time we spend moving every day.

A sedentary lifestyle results in numerous negative effects. Whether you are working every day at a desk or driving a bus or taxi, you are putting yourself at risk of the following problems:

- A higher risk of developing certain cancers
- A greater risk of developing depression and anxiety
- A higher chance of suffering from certain cardiovascular problems
- A greater chance of becoming obese or overweight
- Reduced skeletal muscle mass
- Higher blood pressure
- Raised cholesterol levels

We are more sedentary today than we ever have been in the past because technology has changed how we live our lives. 50 years ago, fewer people used cars and had desk jobs. They also had more physical hobbies and pastimes rather than watching TV and playing video games. Finding ways to counteract the negative impact of the sedentary lifestyle is imperative, but luckily there are several changes you can implement to improve your health, fitness and well-being overall.

We all know that preserving our physical health should be a top priority, but we are also busier than ever before in our lives. With responsibilities such as caring for children or elderly parents, demanding jobs and hectic social life, we are all under pressure in a frantic pace of life. Of course, the most obvious way of getting more active is to go to a gym or to set aside an hour every morning or evening to work out at home.

However, realistically, this just is not possible for some people. Many people are intimidated by the idea of going to the gym, and finding the time to fit physical activity into a daily regime can be virtually impossible. Therefore, finding ways to become more active while going about our regular activities is the best solution.

Here are a few simple hacks to transform your daily routine into a healthier one.

- **Switch to a standing desk rather than a regular one.** Office workers feel tied to their desks for much of the day, but if you make the simple change to standing rather than sitting, you will find that you are less sluggish and stiff when your working day comes to an end. Standing uses a lot more muscles when compared to sitting, and evidence has shown that standing up every 30 minutes and moving around promotes better posture, which in turn reduces tiredness and stress while encouraging better productivity and steadier breathing. If you'd like to take things a step further, why not switch to a treadmill desk instead. This will help you to stay a lot more active while you work, and you can walk or jog at the same time as you carry out your essential work activities.
- **Take the stairs rather than the lift.** Walking up an incline is better for you than walking on a flat surface, so choose the stairs for maximum benefit when getting active. Evidence shows that if you climb the stairs just three times weekly, your cardiorespiratory fitness will improve. Your leg muscles will become stronger and you will also burn more calories for easier bodyweight maintenance.
- **Add simple exercises to your work routine.** If you don't have enough hours in the day to hit the gym, add some muscle workouts into your daily regime instead. Doing squats while at your disk or dips on your office chair won't take much effort,

and it can help you to improve your overall fitness and wellness. You can even add in small changes, such as balancing on one leg while brushing your teeth or doing modified push-ups against your kitchen worktop while you are cooking to improve your health.
- **Ditch the car.** Instead of driving to work or the shop, try biking or walking instead. You will find that it will bring you mental and physical benefits.
- **Use a resistance ball instead of a regular chair.** Whether you are at work or at home, switching your standing chair for a resistance ball will help to automatically straighten your spine, improve your posture and encourage you to stretch and move more often. You can even do some small exercises at the same time, such as modified sit-ups to engage core muscle strength.
- **Take short walks during the day.** During your lunch break, take a quick walk around the block instead. Just a ten-minute walk daily can give you positive mental and physical benefits. A workout doesn't need to take an hour. Just 10 or 15 minutes of physical activity offers benefits too and will not only get your heart pumping but will also help you to improve your mental well-being.

Mindfulness

Rushing about to carry out all your essential tasks can be very stressful, so it is no wonder that more of us find that we've lost our connection with the here and now. Many of us find that we are missing out on the enjoyment of the moment. We overlook the way we are feeling at any given time, and this can lead to negative consequences mentally and physically in our lives. Did you wake up feeling rested today? Did you notice those flowers blooming in your street this morning? Did you hear the birds singing as you arrived at work? If the answer to those questions was no, you should think about practising mindfulness.

Practising mindfulness has been shown to bring a wealth of improvements to both psychological and physical symptoms, helping to bring positive change to attitudes, behaviours and health. When you are mindful, you can enjoy life's pleasures when they occur. This allows you to engage more fully with activities and help you to cope more effectively with negative events in your life. If you focus on the given moment, you will have a reduced chance of getting caught up with your worries about things you have done in the past or things you will do in the future. You will have fewer preoccupations with self-esteem and success while also being able to form better and deeper connections with other people.

Mindfulness has been shown to improve your physical health. It can help to improve heart health, relieve stress, lower your blood pressure, reduce pain, improve your sleep and even alleviate gastrointestinal problems. Meanwhile, it offers a host of mental health benefits, including the relief of depression, anxiety, eating disorders and OCD. Experts believe that, in part, mindfulness works by helping to enable people to accept experiences and emotions instead of reacting with avoidance or aversion.

Mindfulness can be practised in many ways., However, the primary goal of mindfulness techniques is to become more focused and alert yet relaxed by paying close attention deliberately to the sensations and thoughts you experience at any given moment without judgement. As a result, your mind can refocus effectively on the present. There are several different mindfulness techniques. However, this is a basic guide to adding mindfulness practice into your life:

- Start by sitting down quietly and focusing on your breathing patterns. Alternatively, you can focus on a mantra or word which

you repeat to yourself silently. Allow your thoughts to go and come with no judgement, returning every time to focusing on your mantra or breathing.
- Notice the subtle sensations in your body, like tingling or itching. Again, don't judge them; just allow them to pass. Focus your attention on every part of the body, from your head to your toes.
- Notice the sounds, sights, tastes, touches and smells around you. Again, exert no judgement; just allow them to come and go.
- Allow your emotions to stay present but don't judge them. Name your emotions steadily and in a relaxed way. Accept their presence, then allow them to go.
- Cope with your cravings, whether they are for a pattern of behaviours or a substance. Acknowledge the feelings but allow them to pass through you without judgement. Replace your wish for that craving to subside with the knowledge that this will happen eventually.

You can begin practising mindfulness alone by using yoga, tai chi or other concentration meditation methods. You simply need to establish concentration, observe the thoughts, sensations and emotions flowing through your body without judgement, and notice the sensations that you experience. While the process may seem not to be remotely relaxing, with time and practice, you will find that you become happier and more self-aware.

You cannot rush mindfulness. However, the more often you practice, the more you will find that it is effective. Be prepared for the fact that it will usually take about 20 minutes until your mind starts to settle. Practising the above techniques for short periods a few times a week is the best way to start; then, you can work up to longer periods of meditation on more days of the week.

Nutrition

Although we all know that we should eat more whole foods, it can be all too tempting to fall back on the junk food and processed food that we find in restaurants and shops everywhere. Junk food is an ever-present feature of daily life in the world today. The presence of McDonald's, Burger King and KFC up and down the country is simply encouraging more of us to snack on junk from an early age. More people today are eating processed food than ever before, but the trade-off for convenience is a host of health and well-being issues for both the body and mind.

Why is junk food such a problem, and how can it have a negative impact on your well-being? Here, we take a closer look at why whole foods are a better choice in your daily diet and how you can introduce them more effectively into your lifestyle. The definition of junk food is food which is poor in nutrients and dense in calories. Over the past few years, convenience and fast-food consumption have dramatically increased, and today, around a quarter of the population predominantly consumes a processed food diet. As a result, there has been a rising epidemic of chronic diseases.

The main problem associated with the consumption of junk food regularly is obesity. Another complication arising from junk food consumption is the risk of developing diabetes. Insulin levels rise whenever you consume processed sugars which are found in white flour, soft drinks and other food which lacks the essential nutrients and fibre to metabolise carbohydrates effectively. If you eat junk food during the day, your insulin levels can become chronically high, resulting in insulin resistance over time. This causes type 2 diabetes to set in.

If you remove fibre, minerals and vitamins from your diet, you can become nutritionally deficient. This can result in low energy levels, sleep disturbances, low productivity, and mood swings. High levels of sodium found in junk food also result in the overconsumption of salt. This results in heart, kidney and liver diseases as well as hypertension. Not all the complications resulting from the consumption of junk food are physical. Some are mental too. A 2015 study showed that people on high glycaemic diets suffered more from depression than those who had a low GI diet.

Whole foods

Since junk food-heavy diets are so bad for us, it stands to reason that we should look for a better way of eating that promotes well-being and good health. This is where whole foods can come into play. The term "whole foods" is used to refer to food which is closest to its natural state. They are good for us because they bring more nutrients than processed and packaged foods.

Experts suggest that we should all aim for whole foods to make up around 75% of our daily diet. This will help us to stay healthy, free of disease, and with slower ageing. What foods should we be eating? Whole foods include vegetables and fruits which have not been processed, as well as whole grains such as oats, millet, quinoa, cornmeal, buckwheat, rye, and brown rice. We should also be eating more legumes and beans like chickpeas and lentils, as well as more seeds and nuts. Whole foods also include those derived from animal origins, including fish, eggs, seafood, poultry, and lean red meat. If you eat unprocessed foods, you will be able to consume the optimal amount of daily nutrients you require for overall health and well-being in the best possible proportions.

Whole foods contain many different nutrients all in a single food, including minerals, vitamins, fibre, essential fatty acids, and phytonutrients. They are also very rich in substances which cannot be synthesised in the body and which therefore need to be obtained via your diet. For example, valine, an amino acid, cannot be made by the body itself and, therefore, must be supplied via what you eat. It is vital for tissue repair and muscle metabolism, so including plenty of whole foods in your daily regime is essential.

When you eat whole foods in their natural state, you can benefit from the synergy effect of the nutrients in the food working together to benefit your body's healthy functioning. For example, tryptophan, an amino acid, requires B vitamins to be changed into serotonin. Also, whole foods are rich in antioxidants which neutralise free radicals and combat problems like heart disease and cancer.

For many years, experts have been telling us that vegetables and fruits are essential for our well-being. However, many of us still find it difficult to include enough of them in our diets. Yet, whole foods can stop us from becoming ill and help to prevent the problem of obesity. Many studies have revealed that eating more whole foods will supply your body with valuable nutrient sources, including fibre, calcium, magnesium, B vitamins, vitamin D, protein, potassium and essential fatty acids, which ensure your body's cells function in the right way. Foods that are processed are difficult to digest properly and can make you feel sick and tired.

When you add more whole foods into your life, you will experience a host of benefits, including:

- **Improved blood sugar levels.** Processed foods contain insulin growth factor which makes your blood sugar levels higher. As a result, you experience blood sugar swings and cravings. Whole foods won't cause these spikes and will help you to maintain balance throughout the day.
- **Improved digestion.** Whole foods contain lots of fibre which is a vital nutrient for digestion. This fibre is natural and will help you to feel fuller for longer while also supporting your digestion

and lowering your blood sugar levels as it breaks down slowly in the body.
- **Higher energy levels.** The body is more capable of deriving energy from natural foods than processed ones, so you will start to feel more energized with a faster metabolism when you eat more whole foods.
- **Reduced pain.** Processed foods have high inflammatory properties. Since they are acidic in nature, they create pH level imbalances which can result in chronic pain condition symptoms becoming worse. Whole foods keep your body more alkaline and therefore free from inflammation and pain.

Are you convinced of the benefits of eating more whole foods but don't know how to add them to your diet? Here are a few quick tips to point you in the right direction:

- **Switch to traditional oats rather than instant oat cereals.** Instant oats will usually have oat bran removed. This means that a lot of the fibre and vitamins have been removed, reducing its nutritional value.
- **Switch to whole vegetables and fruit rather than packaged juice.** When fruit is juiced, it becomes a concentrated sugar source, and this elevates your blood sugar level much more rapidly when compared with whole fruits. Juicers also remove the skin and pulp of the fruit, so antioxidants and flavonoids are stripped away. Packaged juices also have extra sugar added together with preservatives and chemicals.
- **Switch to fresh fish rather than frozen or canned fish.** Fish contain essential fatty acids that are often removed or reduced during the packaging process. You need omega-3 fatty acids to keep your nervous, immune, reproductive, and cardiovascular systems functioning properly.

You do not need to completely banish all processed food from your life to stay healthy, but if you can increase your whole food consumption to around 75%, you will enjoy much better health and overall well-being.

Probiotics

Most of us tend to think that bacteria are dangerous and bad for us. However, this is not the case. There are many types of bacteria that are beneficial for our bodies. These live micro-organisms are called probiotics, or friendly bacteria, and can help to make your body healthier.

There are different types of probiotics that offer different benefits for your health and well-being. They work in the gastrointestinal tract to boost the immune system, preventing dangerous bacteria from becoming attached to the inside wall of the intestines while improving the function and balance of the intestinal lining's natural microflora. Usually, the human body has an optimal balance of bacteria; however, there are certain lifestyles or medical factors which can create imbalances. As a result, the disease-causing bacteria numbers can grow exponentially.

Unnecessary use of antibiotics, gastrointestinal problems, surgery, chronic stress, and sensitivity to gluten can cause such imbalances. Luckily, there are ways to redress the balance of bacteria for better overall health and well-being. The best way is to include probiotics in your daily diet.

Probiotics is a term used to describe the live bacteria which are present in fermented foods and yoghurt. They can benefit your digestive system by bringing the balance of the bad and good bacteria in your microbiome in alignment. This ensures you have a lower risk of suffering from many different medical conditions and diseases. Probiotics can be derived from natural food sources such as kefir and yoghurt, but they can also be derived from foods which have been enriched with probiotics as well as from specialist supplements. It is usually best to get your probiotics from natural food sources, however.

Probiotics take many forms. Here are some of the most beneficial probiotic foods that you can enjoy every day:

- **Yoghurt** – this is a top probiotic source since it contains milk which has been fermented by good bacteria such as bifidobacterial and lactic acid bacteria. Not only can yoghurt boost your bone health it can reduce high blood pressure and relieve unwanted symptoms associated with IBS (irritable bowel syndrome). Not every type of yoghurt contains probiotics, so you need to choose yoghurts with live or active cultures.
- **Kefir** – this probiotic fermented milk drink is made from goat or cow's milk with added kefir grains. Again, kefir can strengthen the bones, help with digestive issues, and protect the body from infections.
- **Sauerkraut** – this is made from shredded cabbage which has been fermented with lactic acid bacteria. Not only is sauerkraut packed with fibre and vitamins, it also contains manganese, iron and sodium, as well as antioxidants which boost eye health. You need to make sure that the sauerkraut you have chosen is unpasteurized to experience its probiotic benefits.
- **Tempeh** – this product is made from fermented soybeans and is popular as a substitute for meat. The fermentation process means that you can absorb more minerals from tempeh. It is also a rich source of vitamin B12 while also offering probiotic benefits.
- **Kimchi** – this spicy, fermented Korean dish is usually made from cabbage which has been flavoured with chilli pepper, ginger, garlic, salt and scallions. It also contains Lactobacillus kimchi which benefits your digestive health.

- **Miso** – this Japanese seasoning is made from fermented soybeans. Usually made into soup, miso is an excellent source of fibre and protein and is packed with plant compounds, minerals and vitamins.
- **Kombucha** – this fermented green or black tea drink originates from Asia.
- **Pickles** – gherkins are fermented in salt and are an excellent source of probiotic bacteria, which boosts digestive health.
- **Buttermilk** – traditional buttermilk is the liquid that is left behind after making butter. It contains probiotics as well as valuable minerals and vitamins.
- **Natto** – this fermented soybean product is like miso and tempeh, which contains Bacillus subtilis. It is also high in vitamin K2 and protein.
- **Some cheeses** – although many kinds of cheese are fermented, they don't all contain probiotics. Only those that have active and live cultures do. Cottage cheese, cheddar, mozzarella, and gouda are all good examples of cheeses in which good bacteria survive the process of ageing.

There are many probiotic foods which you can add to your diet; however, if you dislike all of them, you could always try a probiotic supplement which can be taken daily to improve your overall health and well-being.

Air

Are you worried about contaminants in the air? Do you suffer from allergic reactions or asthma? Do you have pets in your home, or do you live with a smoker? If the answer to any of these questions is yes, you should consider looking at ways to purify your air. We often believe that the air inside our homes is clean and healthy to breathe., However, it may come as a surprise to learn that it can be just as polluted and contaminated as the air outdoors. Odours, dust, pet dandruff, smoke and mould are just some of the contaminants that you can find in the air inside your home and there are some pollutants inside your home which are present in amounts five times higher than in the air outdoors. It is no wonder, then, that so many people experience allergic reactions and asthma. Finding a way to capture unwanted particles from the air like pollen and dust is vital.

So, how do you know if the air in your home needs purifying? Here are just some of the reasons to consider:

- **You have pets.** If you have a dog or a cat, you could end up suffering from respiratory problems. They shed dandruff onto surfaces of your home, which cannot be removed by vacuuming alone.
- **You suffer from hay fever, asthma, or allergies.** During the spring and summer, hay fever is a common problem due to the pollen particles which are in the air. These irritate the eyes and can cause asthma.
- **You have a mould problem at home.** If your home is humid or prone to dampness, you may find that mould is a problem. Bathrooms and kitchens are problem zones, and without removing the spores from the air, you could develop breathing problems.
- **You have dust mites.** Dust mites are in everyone's home and can cause allergic reactions on the skin as well as breathing problems.
- **You live with a smoker.** Smoke from cigarettes can hang in the air for a long time, causing breathing problems in susceptible individuals, not to mention unpleasant odours.
- **You dislike cooking odours.** Whether you live near neighbours who cook strong-smelling foods or whether you cook

them yourself but don't want the odours lingering around your home, an air purifier can banish the unpleasant smells.
- **You have compromised immunity.** Airborne virus particles can move between individuals when they cough or sneeze.
- **You have a baby.** Young children are especially at risk of airborne viruses and bacteria. They may also be more at risk when they are exposed to harmful contaminants and pollutants in the indoor environment.
- **You live close to a road, agricultural area or industrial facility.** If you live in an area which is at high risk of pollution, you should purify the air inside your home to keep the risk of contamination to a minimum.

As you can see, there are many reasons why you should consider purifying the air in your home to improve your overall health and well-being. There are several things you can do to keep the air in your home clean and pure. One of the best is to invest in an air purifier. This is a device that consists of several filters as well as a fan to suck in the air and circulate it while capturing the particles and pollutants and pushing clean air back to the living space.

When choosing an air purifier, you should make sure to choose one which has a HEPA filter (high-efficiency particulate air filter). These capture particles of a range of sizes in a very fine multi-layered net made from fibreglass threads. This airtight filter ensures that even the tiniest ultra-fine particles are trapped so they cannot be released into the environment to cause problems. You should choose an air purifier that is large enough to effectively clean the air in the space in which you live. This will ensure that the air remains as clean and pure as possible.

There are also some other things you can do to improve the quality of the air inside your home. For a start, although it may sound counter-intuitive, you can keep the windows open, creating a cross-draught whenever possible by opening the window on opposite sides of your rooms. This will ensure that unwanted pollutants and contaminants won't become trapped inside your property, causing your health problems. You should also vacuum your floors frequently to get rid of dust mites which can cause breathing and skin problems. Also, use exhaust fans in your laundry areas, bathroom and kitchen to prevent mould from building up and causing respiratory difficulties and serious illnesses.

You should avoid lighting a wood fire inside your home and avoid smoking inside your property as this will help to boost the quality of air inside your home too. Smoke can cause breathing problems, while second-hand smoke from tobacco can be very harmful to your health, even causing cancer in some cases. Of course, you should also remember to regularly change the filters in your vacuum cleaner, air purifier and ventilation system to ensure that the air indoors stays healthy and clean. A clogged filter cannot readily capture contaminants and particles, so you need to make sure to stay on top of the changing schedule to ensure that maximum pollutants are removed from the air that you and your family breathe every day.

| 10 |

Stress

Stress is a normal response that has kept us safe from danger since pre-historic times. It is what most of us have heard of as the "fight or flight" response, where the perception of threat activates the sympathetic nervous system and triggers an acute stress response that prepares the body to fight or run away. During this stress response, your heart rate and blood pressure increase as adrenaline is released, and the body moves nutrients and oxygen to the major muscle groups. Your body is trying to prioritise so that anything that is not needed for immediate survival, such as the digestive and reproductive systems, temporarily ceases.

Chronic stress

At a low level, stress can be motivating by helping us to achieve things in our everyday lives. The point where stress becomes bad for us is when it becomes excessive and chronic, and the "fight or flight" response is triggered constantly during non-life-threatening situations. Unfortunately, modern lifestyles with urgency and rush contribute to this chronic stress we are likely to feel. This constant release of cortisol, the primary stress hormone, increases the release of glucose into your bloodstream, where it cannot be kept and therefore gets deposited as fat. Over time, the constantly raised blood sugar levels also leave you with an increased risk of Type 2 Diabetes.

Internal stressors on our bodies from injury, chronic illness and gut health can also affect our overall stress levels. Paradoxically, external stress is likely to affect our digestion and cause conditions such as constipation, diarrhoea, stomach ulcers and irritable bowel syndrome. This, in turn, causes its own stress on our bodies and exacerbates our stress levels.

The gut-brain connection

The brain has a direct link to our stomachs and intestines, and this is a two-way link. If we are stressed, the brain sends signals to our gut, and likewise, a troubled gut will send signals to our brain. If our gut is not functioning properly, as we saw in the previous chapter when we looked at healthy gut bacteria, it will send signals to our brain, which can cause anxiety, stress, or depression.

Conversely, stress caused by external factors is likely to influence the physiology of the gut by affecting the movement and contractions of the gastrointestinal tract. Multiple studies have found that finding ways to deal with external stress helps your digestive problems.

Our immune system is also likely to be affected by stress. 80% is housed in the gut wall lining, and when this is not functioning properly, such as due to stress, we are likely to have issues with our immune system. Also, 90% of the happy hormone Serotonin is housed in the gut, and again, if the gut is affected by stress, we are going to experience low moods, such as sadness and depression.

Stress causes energy and blood to be directed away from the areas in the brain that are not needed for "fight or flight", and this will lower our cognitive functioning and our overall performance.

Dealing with stress

Everyone deals with some form of stress in life, and it is not always easy to find relief. Family and work obligations, personal goals, and financial issues can seem never-ending. But there are simple ways to effectively help manage your stress levels so that they don't get to a point where you find yourself crippled by them.

There is no possible way to avoid stress entirely. But there are ways of learning to identify stress triggers, manage stress levels and cope with the stress and anxiety you simply cannot avoid. In this chapter, we will look at just some of the many ways you can improve the quality of your life by learning how to properly manage your stress levels.

Exercise

An easy, natural, yet incredibly powerful method of reducing stress is as simple as putting one foot in front of the other and increasing your day-to-day physical activity levels. Every time we exercise, our bodies naturally release endorphins. These endorphins are hormones that travel throughout our body, giving us a boost of energy and actively ridding the body of stress and anxiety. To get an idea of just how much exercise can improve your mood by releasing these powerful endorphins, take 10 minutes and either walk or jog lightly in place.

Time to reset

In addition to these benefits, exercise can also give you some much-needed alone time so that you can reset your mind and spirit. Whether you are a parent with a full-time job outside of the home, a college student who is constantly surrounded by roommates, or you simply live a hectic, pressure-ridden lifestyle, everyone needs some time by themselves. You will be amazed at how quickly your stress will subside by allowing yourself to recharge.

The digital world

Access to the Internet has brought a lot of good into our world: convenience, social networking, and the ability to work from just about anywhere. But with it comes an extraordinary amount of stress. Think about the last time you sat down to watch your favourite television show. You were probably distracted by your mobile device, which means that you most likely did not absorb everything that you watched. We have become almost numb to the sound of notifications going off on our phones and tablets, incoming emails, alerts, and a myriad of other online signals that pull our attention in a hundred different directions.

If you work online, the constant incoming noise can leave you overwhelmed and stressed. You feel pressured to respond to customers quickly, or perhaps you are trying to manage several different businesses at once and find yourself constantly having to refocus your attention because you have so many things happening at once. It is important to learn to cut out the noise, disconnect and recharge your mental and emotional batteries. Not only will this help you manage stress levels by giving yourself a mental "time out", but ultimately, the downtime will boost creativity levels and help you run your business more efficiently!

The most important time to disconnect from the internet, however, is shortly before we go to bed. Staring at a screen and scrolling has been linked to insomnia-related issues (which lead to high stress levels). For a good night's sleep, turn off all mobile devices about an hour before bedtime. Try reading a magazine or physical book. Do some type of activity that is not too engaging but still somewhat stimulating so that your mind is able to stay focused while still being able to wind down and relax. If you are concerned about someone not being able to get a hold of you in case of an emergency, turn off your notifications in the settings section of your phone and tell people to only call you for emergencies beyond a certain time.

It is important to focus on your own personal downtime every day, even if it is just an extra hour away from the chaos of your business life. There is only so long you can move at a rapid pace before getting burned out, so learning to set a schedule and sticking to it will ensure you are always performing at your very best.

Sleep

Another natural way to reduce stress is to ensure that you get enough, but not too much, sleep. As we saw in the previous chapter when we don't rest enough at the end of our day, our body can tense up, and it leads to irritability and depression. And when we are irritable or depressed, we are stressed. Getting the perfect night's sleep is an easy and natural way to keep stress at bay!

Caffeine

Many adults are self-professed caffeine addicts, and studies now show that coffee does come with some health benefits. But as with everything in life, moderation is key. For some people, caffeine may not be a good idea at all. Everyone has a different caffeine threshold. Some people can handle a lot, some just a little, and some not at all. It all comes down to your body's overall chemistry. Reducing your caffeine intake, be it in the form of coffee or other high-caffeinated beverages, is a natural way to reduce and relieve stress. Just as many of us need caffeine to function after waking up, too much can make us jittery.

If you would like to try cutting back on your caffeine intake, it is important to do so in moderation. Caffeine can be addictive, and going cold turkey can lead to withdrawal symptoms. Try cutting back just one cup a day and see how you feel. Depending on the outcome, keep doing this until you find your threshold. Who knows, you may find that you don't need caffeine at all.

Self-care

So many of us are afraid to say no when people reach out for help, advice and support, and not considering whether saying "yes" is good for us can easily lead to incredibly high stress levels.

- Are you someone who often takes on more than you can handle?
- Are you finding yourself emotionally and mentally depleted because you give so much of yourself to others?
- Are you struggling through toxic relationships that don't add any value or happiness to your life?

And being a "yes" person doesn't just apply to your personal life, but quite often "yes" people are the same way with their jobs or careers. They don't want to miss out on an opportunity, so they sign on for as many tasks or projects as possible. They are worried they will fall behind the competition, so they say yes to every marketing strategy or new course that pops up online, claiming to help them enhance their business skills.

Sometimes managers will reward hard workers with a higher workload output, assuming they will be motivated by the bonus without any consideration as to whether they will be able to perform consistently at the required level. All of this often backfires since people can only do so much before burning themselves out and depleting themselves of that creative energy and motivation to excel. Even if you are someone who thrives under pressure, we all have a breaking point.

If you find yourself in this situation, take a step back and look over your workload. Ask yourself what you can get done within a reasonable amount of time, and then discuss this with your manager, business partner – or simply yourself! Explain why taking on a heavier workload will cause your current one to suffer in quality. And if you work for yourself, consider restructuring your schedule and reducing your workload by getting rid of the tasks that you don't personally need to do. Learn to delegate or outsource.

If you are a student who is constantly stressed out about your course load, then consider taking on a lighter one next term, or if it is not too late, drop one you are currently enrolled in but that you may not need. Or perhaps you are going to college while also working full-time. Look at the benefits of going part-time, and see if you can rework your budget and make it work. In the long run, these changes might require that you stay in college longer than you expected or change your current living situation, but your mind and body will thank you.

Above all else, be selective with your overall workload and what favours you do for people. Prioritise what household chores need to be done, what bills must be paid right away, and know when to say no. If someone else is asking you for help, chances are they understand what it means to have too much on your plate.

Procrastination

Putting tasks off until the last minute can add a tremendous amount of stress to your life, especially if they're important tasks with a specific deadline. And while it is often hard to get things done in a timely manner, it is not impossible with a regular routine. Whatever tasks you need to accomplish, it is important to write them down on a To-Do list or use an online project manager to help you stay on track. This can be for your personal or work life, or you can even have separate lists for both.

Put the tasks that are most important at the very top of your list, paying close attention to whether they are actually of utmost importance or not (it is easy for us to prioritize the tasks we actually enjoy doing over the ones that truly move the needle in our personal or business lives), and then make your way down the list. Be sure to include due dates, too.

And avoid scheduling tasks back-to-back, leaving chunks of time in between each one. You can use this time to reset or just do something that you enjoy doing. It is important to feed your soul throughout the day, as that is an easy and natural way to relieve stress. For example, if you are responsible for more than one project at your job, prioritise the one with the earliest deadline and put it at the top of your to-do list. Break it down into segments throughout your day, allowing time for coffee breaks and social interaction.

Writers are notorious for producing more words each day by using what are called "sprints". This is where they write steadily for 20 minutes, stop for 5-10 minutes, and then repeat. By breaking up their processes so that while they are in a sprint, they are laser-focused on the task at hand while also knowing that a mental and physical break is coming up, they are able to stay focused while also ensuring they recharge and reset.

The same goes for household chores. If you feel overwhelmed by everything that needs to be cleaned and organised around your home, then create a to-do list or download a household printable that makes it easy for you to keep track of your objectives. This will help you keep track of the progress you have made, so you are not feeling overwhelmed. Then work your way down the list to the very last chore that needs to be done.

Remember that when we are stressed, it often affects how we think, and that will reflect in our work. Quite often, we realise far too late that pushing ourselves beyond our mental capabilities results in not only poor output and quality but also taking longer to do simple tasks because we are not giving ourselves a chance to recharge.

Music

When you think about reducing your stress levels, you probably also think about peace and quiet. And while silence can be calming, there are genres of music that can promote tranquillity and inner peace, which result in lower stress levels. When it comes to lowering blood pressure and heart rate, turn to slow-paced instrumental music. For example, classical music with violins or a piano can be very comforting. The soothing sounds will help you feel relaxed and grounded.

And, of course, you can also unwind with the sounds of nature. If you live near a wooded area that is quiet, go outside, close your eyes for a few minutes, and just listen. Picture in your mind the sounds of birds chirping at each other. If this is not an option, then simply search for "nature music" online and see what comes up.

Food

A diet full of processed foods can increase stress levels in our bodies. Unless you immediately channel all those carbohydrates into fuel, such as for a workout, they can easily turn into insulin and wreak havoc on our systems. So, if your diet is relatively high in sugar, consider cutting back and seeing how much it helps your stress levels. When you do cut back on refined carbohydrates, you are bound to feel significantly less sluggish.

Valerian root

A natural supplement that can help reduce your stress levels is valerian root. It is so effective, in fact, that it is often referred to as Nature's Valium. This non-habit-forming herb has a tranquilising effect that aids in getting a good night's sleep. The valeric acid found within valerian root prevents the breakdown of GABA, which is exactly what the anti-anxiety medications Valium and Xanax do. In addition to that, valerian root also contains the antioxidant Hesperidin and Linaria. These antioxidants actually inhibit excessive activity in the amygdala, which is part of our brain that responds to stress with fear.

Stretching

Remember to stretch throughout the day, too, as tense muscles will only add to stress levels. Make sure you have the right mattress for your body type and determine how much sleep you need. Above all else, the most important thing is to keep everything balanced and to try not to overwhelm yourself by taking on more.

| 11 |

Positive Relationships

From the moment you were born, you had an instant relationship with your parents, siblings, and extended family members. When you went to school, you had classmates. When you went to work, you had colleagues and co-workers. You will go through your entire life building and maintaining friendships with a lot of people.

A sense of belonging is a fundamental human need, and loneliness is one of the main causes of depression and even suicide. A study by Harvard University found that the longest predictor of a long and happy life is whether individuals have quality relationships in their lives.

Unfortunately, not all relationships are going to be happy and positive. In fact, you will probably have your fair share of toxic relationships with people around you; this includes your closest family members and friends. If you want to live a happy life, you need to spend less and less time with these toxic individuals. If you can afford to cut them out of your life altogether, do it. It may be hard, but if it is for the best, that is, living your life without them will make you happy, then go for it. Sometimes, a clean break is all you need to push your happiness meter from empty to full.

When you are with the right kind of people (the good kind), your happiness will be off the charts. You will be happier, more inspired, and more likely to be content. Spending your time with good people is literally going to be the highlight of your day, or even your week or month if you don't spend nearly as much time with them as you would like.

Here are a few ways to start building positive relationships with the people around you:

- **Get to know others**
  If you are the shy type, then it is time to start getting out of your shell. Take the initiative and start talking to people. Say something nice and try to build rapport and see if you can get a conversation going. Some probably would want to be left alone. But for most people, having someone else initiate the conversation brings them out of their shell, too. Enjoy making a new friend!
- **Be understanding**
  Whether you like it or not, one of the best ways you can build relationships with others is to be more understanding. Try being open-minded when meeting new people. After all, we all have our differences. We are unique individuals with our own attitudes, our own beliefs, our own cultures. When you are more understanding, you can put yourself in their place.
- **Listening**
  Listening is so much more than just being someone's sounding board. Listen to what the person is saying by being present and paying attention by focusing on the conversation.
  Try to understand what is being said instead of just nodding absentmindedly. Good listeners make great friends; it shows you truly care about the other person.
- **Communication**
  A lot of problems can arise when communication lines get

crossed. This is why it is essential to develop your communication skills. It is so easy to assume everyone understands what you are saying, when in fact, they are taking it the wrong way.

Relationships can quickly go sour because of this. You are saying one thing, but the other person is interpreting it in an entirely different manner.

Happiness

Positive relationships do so much for us. The more positive relationships you have, the happier you will generally be. Happy relationships build our self-esteem and help us go through the motions of life in a more positive state. This, in turn, has the desirable effect of making you enjoy life more.

| 12 |

Conclusion

This book has taken us on a journey, discovering how different areas of our lives impact our well-being, which has an overriding effect on our chances of success.

We saw that engagement and using our strengths to our advantage, rather than focusing on our weaknesses, will improve our well-being and be more successful. Having meaning and purpose in our lives and living according to our values will inspire and motivate us to greater success. Setting appropriate goals that challenge us without being so unachievable that they demotivate us is another way of achieving success. A growth mindset rather than limiting beliefs helps us reframe negativity and increase self-esteem, a major contributor to sub-optimal performance. We went on to look at success and how decision-making and consistency affect our performance and well-being. Closely related to this is motivation, which also has a major impact on our chances of success. Positive emotions and happiness are major factors in our well-being, and we explored the effect on this of gratitude and kindness. We then looked at the various aspects of our health, including nutrition, exercise, sleep and stress on our well-being and performance levels. Finally, we saw how positive relationships and belonging are key to our well-being.

By now, it will have become clear that there is no single "fix" for improving our well-being and success. I started the book by mentioning that well-being is multi-faceted, and we have seen how there are so many overlaps in how different areas of our lives interact both positively and negatively towards our aim for optimum well-being and success. It is certainly possible to achieve optimum well-being and success by improving the different areas we have discussed. However, for most of us, it will be a work in progress over many years, and as we have also seen, we should not let that become a de-motivator just because we do not achieve instant results in all areas.

Use the goal-setting advice to plan the areas that need improving and remember to note why you want to achieve the improvement, and in due course, you will reach your goal of well-being and improved performance.

I wish you every success!

Key exercises from each Chapter
Well-being:
PERMAH survey and PERMAH wheel
Engagement:
Strengths Usage Journal
Meaning:
Personal Mission Statement
Accomplishment and Goal-setting:
Hope Map
Growth Mindset:
Positive Affirmations

Success:
Three Good Things Journal
Motivation:
Vision Board
Positive Emotions:
Positivity Ratio
Health:
Review current lifestyle

Anna Barwick started her career as an award-winning Chartered Certified Accountant, before becoming a successful business entrepreneur. After a life-threatening immune system collapse left her hospitalised, she discovered positive psychology and realised that, after applying it to her own life, she became not only more successful but was much happier in the process!

She went on to study to become a certified positive psychology coach to allow her to help other entrepreneurs benefit from her experience, and was voted Business Coach of the Year 2022-23.

www.ingramcontent.com/pod-product-compliance
Lightning Source LLC
Chambersburg PA
CBHW072052110526
44590CB00018B/3134